# EVEREST

*THE HISTORY*
*OF THE HIMALAYAN GIANT*

1 *Prayer banners fly at the Rongbuk monastery in Tibet whilst in the background rises the mighty North Face of Everest.*
Photo by Galen Rowell/ Mountain Light Photography

2-3 *The Tibetan side of Everest, facing north, is surrounded by the great streams of the Rongbuk Glacier; on the left of the photo can be seen the imposing bulk of the Changtse (or North Peak).*
Photo by Mark Shapiro/ D. Perret-J. Troillet

4-5 *Tracks in the snow left by the porters and climbers of a French expedition in the late Eighties snake along the slopes leading to the North Col (Chang-La).*
Photo by René Robert/ Agenzia Freestyle

6-7 *One of the climbers from the French expedition led by Marc Batard in the autumn of 1990 climbing towards Camp III along the usual Nepalese route.*
Photo by Pascal Tournaire

8-9 *At the center of the photo, beyond the Nuptse crest, rises the imposing rocky Southwest Face of Everest.*
Photo by Jean Michel Asselin/Vertical

9 *Christine Janin tackling the summit crest of Everest. The date is the 5th of October 1990, and the French climber is completing the first stage of the "Top Seven" —ascents of the highest peaks on the seven continents.*
Photo by Pascal Tournaire

# CONTENTS

*10-11 Following a
number of days of bad
weather and blizzards,
the final section of the
North Face of Everest
has an almost wintry
appearance.
Photo by Mark Shapiro/
D. Perret-J. Troillet*

*12-13 September 1975.
Having left Camp VI,
the British climber
Dougal Haston climbs
along the rope railing
of the Upper Snowfield on
the Southwest Face.
Photo by Doug Scott*

**Texts**
Roberto Mantovani

**Introduction**
Kurt Diemberger

**Editorial Coordination**
Laura Accomazzo

**Layout**
Patrizia Balocco Lovisetti
Clara Zanotti

English translation reviewed by William Fortney

© 1997 White Star S.r.l.
Via Candido Sassone, 22/24
13100 Vercelli, Italy.

This edition published in 1997 by

The Mountaineers
1001 SW Klickitat Way
Seattle, WA 98134

Produced by: White Star S.r.l.
Via Candido Sassone, 22/24
13100 Vercelli, Italy.

ISBN: 0-89886-534-4

Printed in the month of August
1997 by Grafedit, Bergamo
(Italy).
Color separation
Fotolito Graphic Service, Milan
Tecnolito, Caprino Bergamasco,
(Bergamo).

10 9 8 7 6 5 4 3 2 1

Chomolungma, the Goddess Mother of the World for the Tibetans (for Westerners, more simply Everest), the highest obelisk in the terraqueous world—just under 9,000 meters high—has long been for mankind one of the last areas of mystery in a world insistently ransacked in its most secret nooks and crannies. Exactly as happened with the Poles and the last scraps of *terra incognita*, the epic story of Everest began even before the eyes of any explorer or climber succeeded in viewing the mighty outlines of the Himalayan giant. Announced for some time, expected for even longer, the "discovery" of the highest mountain in the world had occurred thanks to science and technology—the trigonometric calculations and theodolites of the British topographers in the Survey of India. And from the very start, in the Western world, it had triggered off that subtle vertigo which always comes over man when faced with an unknown reality. A strange unease, which can be overcome

exploration fever. Understandably, because in that period the Himalayan adventure was taking place in regions which were completely unknown and uncharted. But an explanation of this kind is not enough, it is too limited. We must in fact bear in mind that, in the first decades of the twentieth century, the world of high mountains constituted for urban society and Western technology a magnificent opportunity— one of the last—to peer into the uncertain territory of the imaginary and undefined, where the density of the air is different from the rest of the planet, and hypoxia and fatigue cause climbers to hallucinate.

Only much later, explorers' outfits cast aside, did climbing in the Himalayas, or Everest, recover its sporting dimension. From 1975 on, in less than two decades, practically all the faces and ridges of "the roof of the world" have been climbed by mountaineers. In some cases even without the aid of breathing equipment and oxygen, following a

# $\mathcal{P}$REFACE

in one way only: by making the unknown known. By using, that is, the same mechanism, the same curious tendency of the human spirit which, from the most ancient times, has accompanied the discovery and exploration of new lands. For a long time, the idea of scaling that towering summit in the Himalayas had remained in the background, confined to the evanescent universe of dreams. Only in the second decade of the twentieth century did the plan to climb Everest become reality, although the first attempts seemed still affected by the

route already traced by pre-war British pioneers and then definitively inaugurated in 1978 by Reinhold Messner and Peter Habeler.

Today, in the era of commercial expeditions, of the race to the summit along the normal routes, of the overcrowding of the base camps, the discovery of a new, logical and quite independent route on Everest seems quite impossible. It is hard, on the threshold of the third millennium, to find something truly new: there are already too many routes. Some parts which are still unexploited remain, for example the central part of the Yellow Band on the north side, which presents a less than commonplace problem, but not much else. In the immediate future the great routes of the recent past might be repeated in the Alpine style—someone has already thought of this. But the attraction of relaunching the game in a different way and climbing where no one has ever been is another thing.
An "impossible" dream, a sort of present for Himalayan climbers of the year 2000 would be a traverse linking Nuptse, Lhotse and Everest. For the moment a splendid madness, tomorrow who knows.

*14 The northern side of Everest (Chomolungma to the Tibetans) rises majestically above the Rongbuk Glacier.*
Photo by Mark Shapiro/
D. Perret-J. Troillet

*14-15 The warm light of sunset bathes the pyramidal peak of Everest, throwing into sharp relief walls, crests and gullies.*
Photo by Jean Michel
Asselin/Vertical

16-17 *Two climbers ascending through the labyrinthine seracs of the Ice Fall, even today one of the most dangerous stretches of the classic Nepalese route to the summit of Everest.* Photo by Jean Michel Asselin/Vertical

"Papa, how come you've never climbed Everest?" my daughter Hildegard asked me, almost with a note of slight reproach. Modern times, we might say. "All your friends have—why haven't you?" she continued. "I don't know," I replied. "Now I'm going to climb Makalu, which attracts me more." Why haven't I climbed Everest yet? As if everyone had to climb Everest just because it's the highest. Modern times, I thought.

But when I said that, I had not yet seen Everest.

And I did not know that both Hildegard and I, each in our different ways, were destined to end within the magic circle of Chomolungma, the "Goddess Mother of the World."

I changed my mind when I was confronted with the mountain for the first time in spring 1974, and saw the highest peak in the world, in the midst of her fabulous court, from a completely unusual angle, from the "hidden valley" of Barun. Then it showed me a secret

*18 top  A climber ascending towards the Raphu-La where the interminable Northeast Ridge begins. The ridge route was completed in its entirety for the first time by a Japanese expedition in May 1995.*
Photo by Kurt Diemberger

*18 bottom left  Struggling with a heavy Arriflex, Kurt Diemberger, climber and filmmaker, is taking a panoramic shot near Camp III on the Lhotse Face.*
Photo: Kurt Diemberger Archive

*18 bottom right The French climber Nicolas Jaeger smiles for Kurt Diemberger's camera shortly after having reached the summit of Everest on the 15th of October 1978.*
Photo by Kurt Diemberger

*19  A climber ascending a fixed rope along the chaotic Khumbu serac (the Ice Fall), near Camp I on the classic Nepalese route.*
Photo by Pat Morrow

# $\mathcal{I}$NTRODUCTION
## BY KURT DIEMBERGER

side, never seen in photographs—I had the feeling of seeing a group of immense crystals touching the sky, a unique constellation rising in incredible splendor above the dark valley. Dumb, silent, yet dynamic. Like crests of gigantic waves rising ever higher in single crystalline tips as they grow mightily out of the ocean, they stood there, in the sky—immobile, spellbound in a split second of time as if by a magic word.

At the same time there was something infinitely soft and gentle in the snow, as if that magnificent mountain had a merciful soul.

I realized in that second why the Tibetans saw her as "the goddess mother," and also as the "mistress of the continent"—because she emitted understanding together with a severe grandeur in her imposing appearance.

For the Tibetans there was no sense in splitting up the great personality: for them that whole complex of peaks I was admiring was "Chomolungma." Only the cartographers felt the need to give a name to every crest in the Everest group (which was named after the head of the Indian Survey, then in British hands).

It is, however, just as well for climbers, if they can identify the peaks they see on the map . . .

In fact, in the foreground of the group in front of me Lhotse, the "South Peak" (lho = south, tse = peak), rose in an enormous 8,511-meter rock face among very steep ridges and vertical angles, while to its right, at some distance, I could make out the white shape of Shartse, the "East Peak" (shar = east), a virgin Seven Thousander, never yet attempted but which I hoped to climb with my friends. Glued to the sky behind the line of the great ridge, which from there continued towards Lhotse, was the highest peak, the unmistakable pyramid of Everest, which completely hid Changtse, or "North Peak," another Seven Thousander. To the left of Lhotse, another ice giant hid Nuptse, the "West Peak" of the group, from my sight.

I could not complain: in all that immense agglomerate of towering peaks I could admire another Eight Thousander, a prohibitive peak right next to Lhotse, a little to the east, 8,383 meters high . . . the poor cartographers, having used up the names of the four directions of the

wind, called it (they could hardly do otherwise) Lhotse Shar, that is, more or less "East of South Peak."

Be that as it may, as far as I know, the naming story is not finished yet. Along the vast crest another Seven Thousander follows on, Peak 38, a little further east from the previous peak but at the same time also a little further west of Shartse (Until now no one has dared to think up a new name for the latest incognito!).

The Tibetan view of "Chomolungma" is definitely less complicated, but climbers and geographers are keen on precision.

And they have their reasons.
For me the first sight of the group was a real adventure, and the beginning of five expeditions to Everest, during which I was once on the summit, but this is not the only thing which counts. I have lived with this mountain—I know it now from every side—and Everest has not only allowed me to discover many of her hidden valleys and highest ridges but has also enabled me to take part in the lives of the people of those places where the expeditions pass. She has

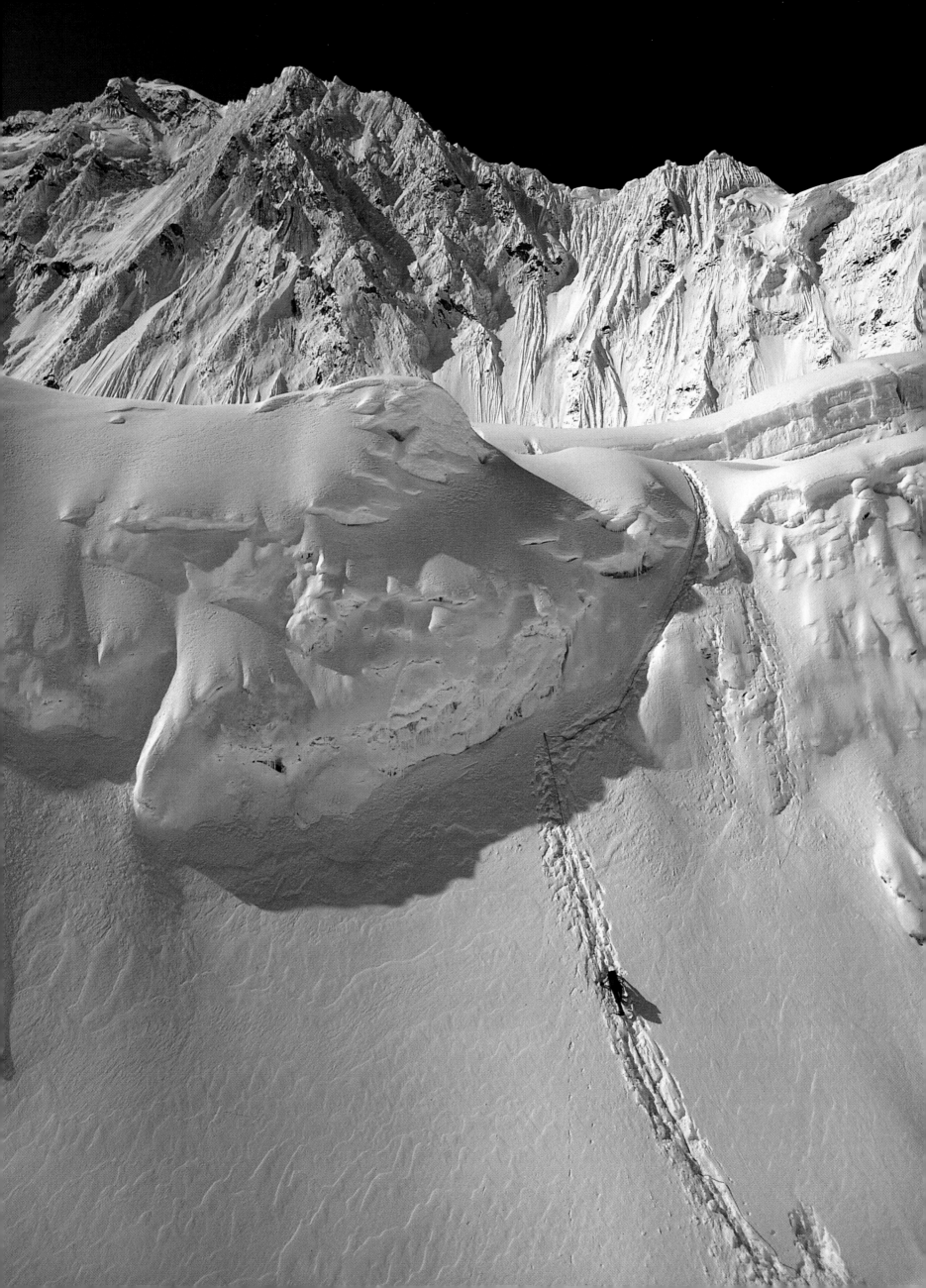

taught me to live at high altitudes and given me many human experiences. In a certain sense, if I think of my career as a high altitude cameraman, she has also decidedly transformed my life.

And not lastly, she has made me dream. Even then, in 1974, our goal was not simply the first ascent of that virgin, 7,502-meter-high peak, Shartse. As we took the first steps on the "Great Crest of Everest," that immense "over two thousand" traverse, we felt like pioneers. If someday a successful crossing of the whole group is made—from Shartse across the summits of Peak 38, Lhotse Shar, and Lhotse, down to the South Col, up over the summit of Everest itself, down into Tibet to the North Col, concluding with Changtse—it will take the joint partnership of several expeditions and also a great deal of luck with the weather. Dreams of the future, of course, but I think one day it will be possible.

One of my vocations has been to arouse the enthusiasm of others for that world of Everest, bringing its marvels back with me. I have shot six films on Chomolungma and its people, the last with my daughter, Hildegard, an ethnologist, in the winter of 1993, on the Tibetans living to the northeast of the mountain.

Roberto Mantovani (together with others who know Everest) has given a wide picture of the development of events—as well as a kaleidoscopic view of the mountain from every side with the best photographs imaginable—however I think that it is worth relating some observations from my personal experience.

In 1978 when I shot the high altitude sequences for the French film right up to the summit, I was part of a traditional expedition, in siege style, with many high altitude porters, fixed ropes, the use of oxygen cylinders. At the same time Doug Scott and two friends were undertaking an attempt on Nuptse in pure Alpine climbing style. The reader, who is sure to know that many climbers have made the ascent without oxygen, will perhaps smile at this old system, judging it out of date. Even the expeditions that use oxygen today hardly mention it in their reports. But does the reader have any idea of what it really means to carry that blessed oxygen on one's back? Cylinders today are much lighter not only than the "British air" of 1922 but also than the more modern ones used in the French expedition. Following up an observation I made in my book *The Spirits of the Air*, I would like the

In the twenty years that went by between this enterprise and my first experience of Everest, the ascent of Shartse in 1974, many things have changed in the Himalayas. There has been a rapid evolution, with its positive sides of course, but also with negative effects: specifically the impact on the local populations and, in the strictly climbing field, the racing and competition that have started here, although on Everest you can still find all climbing styles. I do not think this is the place to undertake a broad discussion on the subject, especially since an expert like

reader to reflect on the fact that a Russian titanium cylinder in use in the 1990s weighs from 2.2 to 3.3 kilos, compared to the 7 kilos typical in the 1970s, or more than 15 kilos of earlier cylinders and regulators, and that this "modern" reduction in weight (about 50%) is a not negligible factor for the "traditional" ascents of today. In a very few years no one will be able to appreciate the effort made by Edmund Hillary and Tenzing Norgay during their first ascent—before their route became what today looks like a crowded highway.

When Hillary came with us to the East Face of Everest in 1981 as member of an American team (of which I was film director), climbing techniques had already made enormous progress. Otherwise we should never have been able to climb the vertical wall of rock under the "ice monster," a dangerously sheer precipice with enormous stalactites menacing our way— the only route possible given the many avalanches on the East Face. Despite everything, the first thousand meters of ascent, the so-called "buttress," used up all our time, as well as our

20 One is truly in the hands of fate in the Khumbu serac at an altitude of 6,000 meters. Vast blocks of ice as large as entire buildings may fall from one moment to the next.
Photo by Kurt Diemberger

20-21 A number of climbers rapidly crossing the Ice Fall. The unstable labyrinth of seracs is an obligatory stage for those following the classic Nepalese route.
Photo: Mountain Equipe Archive

21 top In recent years the route that from the North Col rises to join the Northeast Ridge and on to the summit of Everest has been tackled by innumerable expeditions.
Photo by Jean Michel Asselin/Vertical

21 bottom Pierre Mazeau tackling the Hillary Step (on the classic Nepalese route), the final obstacle before the summit of Everest. He is preceded in the distance along the ice cornice by Jean Afanasieff and Nicolas Jaeger.
Photo by Kurt Diemberger

nerves and a great deal of energy. After overcoming the key passage on the route, we raised the white flag—also because of the considerable danger of avalanches on the easy slopes we would have to cross on our ascent.

Two years later, with the help of a rocket, the Americans set up transport with cables over the above-mentioned vertical face—then, having established the camps, they reached the summit. Since then, only Stephen Venables, with two companions, has succeeded in finding a way up the east side of Everest. But it is not over yet.

The "artist ridge" remains, awaiting someone! I baptized it so, placing two mini-paintings by an artist friend of mine in the crack of a tower of rock at the foot, and then admired the procession of ghostly figures of ice following each other along the top of the ridge! But I think no one will make this trek.

The East Face of Everest, with its constant fall of avalanches, in 1921 had inspired George Mallory and his companions with awe, making them decide to seek an ascent on the north side. Then in 1924 George Mallory and Sandy Irvine

vanished among the clouds near the summit. Thirty years later, Hillary and Tenzing made their historic ascent from the south side, but no one will ever know whether Mallory and Irvine reached the summit before them.

Subsequently two great climbers have written their names in the history book of Everest: Reinhold Messner and Peter Habeler. In the spring of 1978 they succeeded in achieving the first ascent without the aid of oxygen. Then another rope party, Erhard Loretan and Jean Troillet, climbed the north side in the purest

Alpine style, without even a tent, simply carrying a shovel to dig a hole in the snow to bivouac.

On the south side every attempt to climb light has been frustrated by the Khumbu Ice Fall. The Alpine style purists here had to set their ideologies a little to one side, make a compromise, and begin Alpine style above it. This is what Messner did in 1980, when he came here during the Italian expedition, of which I was also a member. It was not a good time for him or for me: although I had lent him my Sherpa to establish his camp on the Lhotse Face, a blizzard blowing for several days cost him and me the summit. While I was waiting on the South Col to film my companions ascending to the summit of Everest, one of our tents, torn to shreds by the gusts of wind, flew off towards Tibet, and some of my friends suffered from frostbite.

In any case it is impossible for a rope party of only two or three climbers to manage to surmount the enormous ice fall elegantly; about eight hundred—or perhaps almost one thousand—meters high, it is in continual movement and advances at the speed of one meter a day. I have seen so many broken aluminum ladders, heard so many prayers from the Sherpas, and said quite a few myself!

There are whole plateaus of the glacier which slide forwards and shift over cavities— they lie suspended over a void—until their weight is too much and the whole plateau in a few seconds smashes into thousands of pieces. If anyone finding himself on such a plateau (which can even be the size of a football field!) is not crushed between the blocks of ice, he may thank his lucky stars! There were two deaths in 1980, a Sherpa, Nawang Kenzang, died exactly in that way, while the climber Franco Piana was dragged by a snowslide into a crevasse in the side of Lhotse. The so-called "normal route" up Everest will always be one of the most dangerous . . . Many forget this.

I would like to go on to happier memories: the amazing climber Doug Scott, who was well aware that the Khumbu Ice Fall cannot be conquered in Alpine style! One day he arrived at our French base camp with a couple of bottles of whiskey and offered them as "a small contribution in exchange for the use of the heavy ladders placed on the serac." His natural attitude was greatly appreciated. As for climbing styles, I think that a difficult route itself determines the technique to use, or at least the most advisable. On the Northeast Ridge of Everest, Chris Bonington recognized that the best protection against the terrible blizzards which scourged that route were caves dug inside the snow and the ice—a great "mole-style" job, which produced very effective "shelters"! In 1985, when Julie Tullis and I were filming the Anglo-Scottish expedition, we used them several times. They were still in good condition, despite the three years that had gone by!

On the "normal routes" up Everest, nowadays so-called "commercial expeditions" move in increasing numbers. Most of them have expert guides, but as for the customers—who knows? They may be competent, but how many of them depend simply on the experience of the guide— and on luck? They do not know each other, they have simply paid, and so there are those who insist, despite the weather conditions, on getting the desired result—which, in their view, was promised to them!

At high altitude, if things do not go smoothly, these people are done for. And the guide, however expert, may risk losing his life. Of course, there may be blizzards which are so terrible at these heights that no one is spared, not even those who have learned how to live up high. But I think that those who want to go, would do well to determine whether they are really up to it and understand that you cannot buy a ticket to the highest mountain in the world as if it were a theater show. Up there you need more than a ticket and climbing gear.

There are many different views even among experts—and this is natural. For me mountains are not there for people to try out a particular technique, at any cost, and even less for people to show off their skills. Mountains ought to be like friends—and we should never forget to respect them! They are not a means to assess ability, but something very different. One should not go on Everest without reflecting. Without seeking to get to know this mountain. To speak to her in silence, perhaps even face to face.

Because Chomolungma is more than just the highest mountain in the world.

*22 In this photo, taken from the Space Shuttle, you can clearly see the huge triangle of the East Face bathed in the early morning light. The North Face is almost entirely shadowed. You can also easily distinguish the Nepalese side of the mountain and the glaciers that surround the massive orographic node.*
Photo: NASA

*23 Drawn by Bradford Washburn, a photographer and geophysicist from the Boston Museum of Science, this map of Everest to 1:50,000 scale is one of the most precise and reliable of the region. It was published by the US National Geographic Society in 1988.*
Photo: National Geographic Society

*24-25 Beyond Camp IV on the saddle of the South Col, the southern peak of Everest, which reaches an altitude of 8,765 meters, rises powerfully in defense of the true peak.*
Photo by Jean Michel Asselin/Agence Freestyle

*26-27 Of vast proportions, the North Face of Everest is incised by two deep gullies, the Great Couloir (or Norton Couloir) on the left and the Hornbein Couloir on the right.*
Photo by Mark Shapiro/ D. Perret-J. Troillet

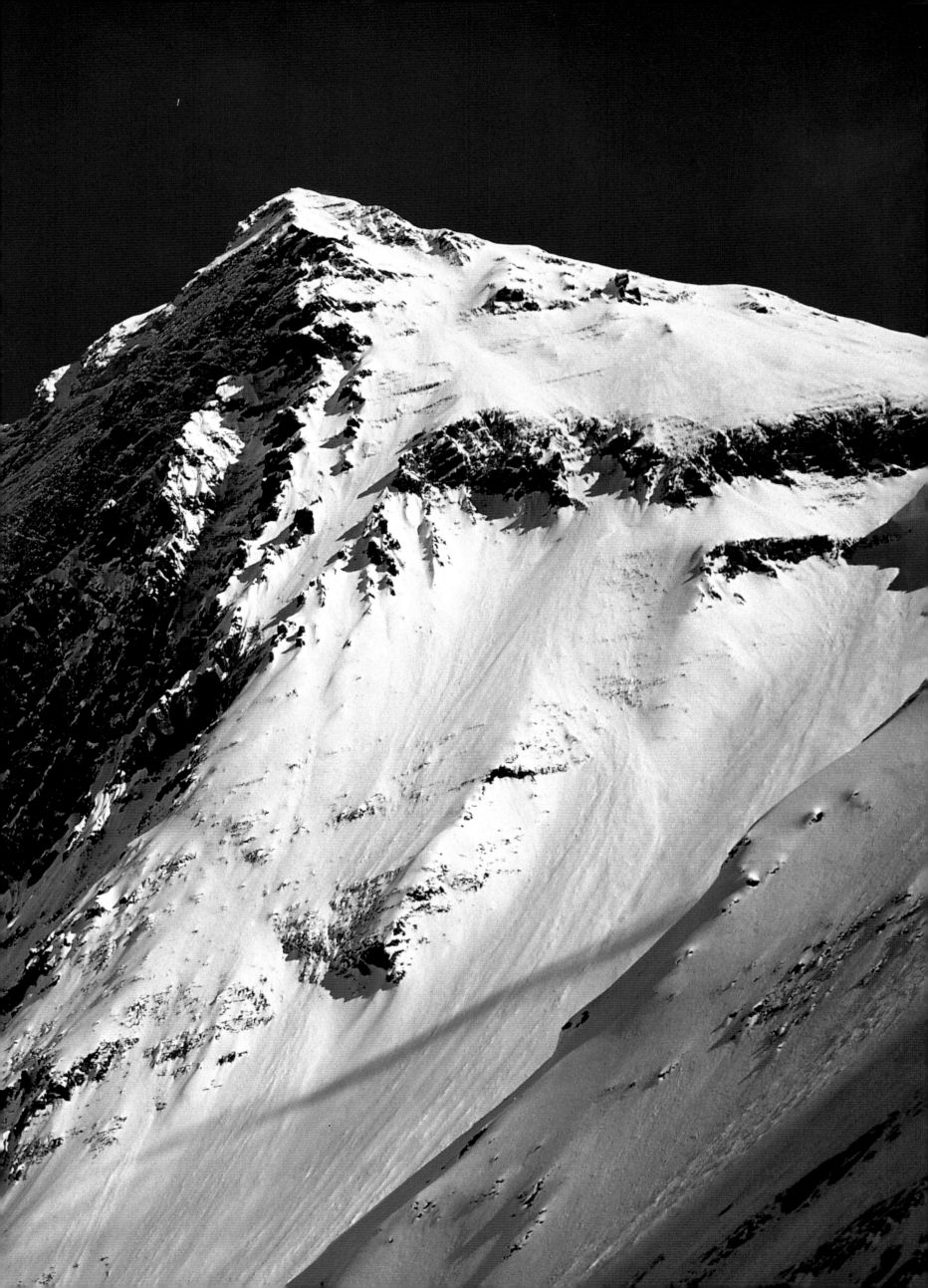

**1953:** first ascent by a British expedition led by H.C.J. Hunt. On 29th May the summit is reached by Edmund Hillary and Tenzing Norgay. The ascent route goes along the Ice Fall, through the Western Cwm, touches the South Col and continues along the Southeast Ridge.

**1956:** a Swiss expedition led by Albert Eggler repeated the original route. On the 23rd of May Jürg Marmet and Ernst Schmied reached the summit; the following day it was the turn of Hans Rudolf von Gunten and Adolf Reist.

**1960:** a Chinese expedition led by Shih Chan-chun scaled the North Col and continued along the North and Northeast Ridges to the summit. On the 25th of May Wang Fu-chou, Chu Yin-hua and a Tibetan named Gonpa reached the summit.

**1963:** an American expedition led by Norman Dyhrenfurth. On the 1st of May James Whittaker and the Sherpa Nawang Gombu reached the summit via the South Col

route. On the 22nd, Luther Jerstad and Barry Bishop repeated the climb. On the same day Tom Hornbein and Willi Unsoeld opened a new route after having covered a section of the West Ridge and continued along a couloir (today known as the Hornbein Couloir) that cuts into the north side, eventually reaching the summit.

**1965:** between the 19th and the 29th of May, 9 climbers from an Indian expedition reached the summit via the 1953 route: A.S. Cheema, Nawang Gombu (his second ascent), Sonam Gyatso, Sonam Wangyal, C.P. Vohra, Ang Kami, Hari Pal Singh Ahluwalia, Harish Chandra S. Rawat, and Phu Dorje.

**1970:** the Saburo Matsukata expedition. An attempt on the Southwest Face and an ascent via the usual South Col route. Terup Matsura and Naomi Uemura reached the summit on the 11th of May; on the following day the ascent was also completed by Katsutoshi Hirabayashi and the Sherpa Chotare.

# ALL THE ASCENTS

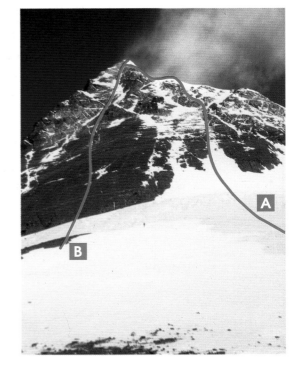

*28 top left  29th May, 1953: Tenzing Norgay reaches the summit of Everest.*
Photo: Royal Geographical Society

*28 bottom left  The 1963 American route followed the West Shoulder, the West Ridge and the Hornbein Couloir* **[A]**.
Photo by Chris Curry/ Hedgehog House

*28 top right  1956: the Swiss climber Jürg Marmet completes the second ascent together with Ernst Schmied.*
Photo by Jürg Marmet

*28 bottom right The British route of 1953 climbed towards the South Summit* **[A]**. *The Polish route to the South Buttress, 1980* **[B]**.
Photo by Andrzej Zawada

**1973:** an Italian expedition led by Guido Monzino along the classic Nepalese route. Rinaldo Carrel and Mirko Minuzzo, together with the Sherpas Shambu Tamang and Lhakpa Tenzing reached the summit on the 5th of May; two days later the climb was repeated by Claudio Benedetti, Virginio Epis, Fabrizio Innamorati and Sonam Gyalzen.

**1973:** a Japanese expedition led by Michio Yuasa, attempted the Southwest Face and the classic South Col route. On the 26th of October the first objective was abandoned; on the same day, however, Hisashi Ishiguro and Yasuo Kato reached the summit after having climbed from the South Col.

**1975:** a Japanese female expedition led by Eiko Hisano, along the classic Nepalese route. Junko Tabei (the first woman to the top of Everest ) reached the summit on the 16th of May together with the Sherpa Ang Tsering.

**1975:** after having climbed to the North Col a Chinese expedition led by Shih Chan-chun took the North Ridge and continued along the Northeast Ridge to the summit. On the 27th of May eight Tibetans (including a woman) and a Han Chinese climber reached the summit: Phanthog (second woman to climb Everest), Sonam Norbu, Lotse, Samdrub, Darphuntso, Kunga Pasang, Tsering Tobgyal, Ngapo Khyen, Hou Sheng-fu.

**1975:** a British group led by Chris Bonington completed the first ascent of the Southwest Face. On the 24th of September Dougal Haston and Doug Scott reached the summit, followed, two days later, by Pete Boardman, the Sherpa Pertemba and (probably) by Mick Burke.

**1976:** an Anglo-Nepalese expedition led by Tony Streather, along the classic South Col route. Michael Lane and John Stokes reached the summit on the 16th of May.

**1976:** an American expedition led by Philip Trimble. Classic Nepalese route. Chris Chandler and Robert Cormack reached the summit on the 8th of October.

**1977:** South Korean expedition led by Kim Young Do. Ko Sang-Do and the Sherpa Pemba Norbu reached the summit on the 15th of September.

**1978:** Austrian expedition led by Wolfgang Nairz.

**1979:** integral ascent of the West Ridge by a Yugoslavian expedition led by Tone Skarja. Andrej Stremfelj and Jernej Zaplotnik reached the summit on the 13th of May followed, two days later, by Stane Belak, Stipe Bozic and the Sherpa Ang Phu (his second ascent of Everest).

**1979:** German expedition led by Gerhard Schmatz. Classic Nepalese route. At the summit on the 1st of October: the Germans Gerhard Schmatz and Hermann Warth, the Swiss Hans von Känel, and the Sherpas Lhakpa Gyalzo and Pertemba (his second ascent of Everest). The climb was repeated the following day by the American Ray Genet, the Germans Hannelore Schmatz, Günther Kämpfe and Tilman Fischbach, the New Zealander Nick Banks and the Sherpas Sundare, Ang Phurba and Ang Jangbo.

**1980:** Polish expedition led by Andrzej Zawada. Classic Nepalese route. First winter ascent completed on the

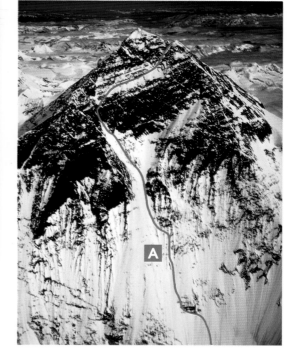

Classic Nepalese route. Wolfgang Nairz, Robert Schauer, Horst Bergmann and the Sherpa Ang Phu reached the summit on the 3rd of May. On the 8th of May, Reinhold Messner and Peter Habeler completed the first ascent of Everest without oxygen. Three days later the ascent was repeated (with oxygen) by the German Reinhard Karl and on the 14th of May by Oswald Ölz and Franz Oppurg.

**1978:** German expedition led by Karl Herrligkoffer. Classic Nepalese route. Sepp Mack, Hubert Hillmaier and Hans Engl reached the top on the 14th of October. Two days later, the climb was repeated by the Pole Wanda Rutkiewicz, the Swiss Robert Allenbach, the Germans Sigi Hupfauer and Willi Klimek, and the Sherpas Mingma Dorje, Ang Dorje, and Ang Kami. Lastly, on the 17th of October, the Germans Georg Ritter and Bernd Kullmann also reached the summit.

**1978:** French expedition led by Pierre Mazeaud. Classic Nepalese route. At the summit on the 15th of October: Jean Afanassieff, Nicolas Jaeger, Pierre Mazeaud, and Kurt Diemberger.

17th of February by Leszek Cichy and Krzysztof Wielicki.

**1980:** a Japanese expedition led by Hyoriko Watanabe opens a new direct route on the North Face, climbing along the upper section of the Hornbein Couloir. Takashi Osaki and Tsuneoh Shigehiro reached the summit on the 10th of May. Also of note was the solo climb by Yasuo Kato (his second ascent of Everest), along the Northeast Ridge.

**1980:** Basque expedition led by Juan-Ignacio Lorente. Classic Nepalese route. At the summit on the 14th of May: Martin Zabaleta and the Sherpa Pasang Temba.

**1980:** Polish expedition led by Andrzej Zawada. First ascent of the South Spur. Jerzy Kukuczka and Andrzej Czok reached the summit on the 19th of May.

**1980:** climbing solo on the 20th of August, Reinhold Messner opened a new route on the North Face. The route partially followed the Northeast Ridge, crossed the North Face and continued along the Great Couloir.

*29 left  The Chinese route of 1960* **[A]**. *The Yugoslavian route on the West Ridge in 1979* **[B]**. *The Japanese route of 1980* **[C]**. *The Messner variant on the North Face, 1980* **[D]**.
Photo by Mark Shapiro/D. Perret–J. Troillet

*29 top right  On the 22nd of May 1963, the American climber Tom Hornbein opened a new route together with Willi Unsoeld.*
Photo by Tom Hornbein

*29 bottom right  The Southwest Face, the route followed by the Bonington expedition in 1975* **[A]**.
Photo by Keiichi Yamada/Chris Bonington Picture Library

**1981:** in the autumn, an American expedition led by John B. West traced a variant on the classic South Col route, linking the South Buttress (the Polish route) with the Southeast Ridge (classic Nepalese route). At the summit on the 21st of October: Chris Kopczynski and the Sherpa Sundare (his second ascent of Everest). Three days later the climb was repeated by Peter Hackett, Chris Pizzo, and the Sherpa Yong Tenzing.

**1982:** a Russian team led by Evgeny Tamm, opened a difficult new route on the buttress to the left of the Southwest Face. Between the 4th and the 9th of May, 11 climbers reached the summit: Eduard Myslovsky, Sergei Bershov, Vladimir Balyberdin, Mikhail Turkevich, Valentin Ivanov, Sergei Yephimov, Kazbek Valiev, Valeri Khrishchaty, Yuri Golodov, Vladimir Puchkov and Valeri Khomutov.

**1982:** Canadian expedition led by William March. Classic Nepalese route. At the summit on the 5th of October: Laurie Skreslet,with the Sherpas Lhakpa

**1983:** Japanese expedition, led by Hiroshi Yoshino. Classic Nepalese route. At the summit on the 8th of October: Haruyuki Endo, Hiroshi Yoshino and Hironobu Kamuro.

**1983:** Japanese winter expedition led by Kazuyuki Takahashi. Classic Nepalese route. At the summit on the 16th of December: Takashi Ozaki (his second ascent of Everest), Noboru Yamada, Kuzunari Murakami and the Sherpa Nawang Yonden.

**1984:** Bulgarian expedition led by Avram Iliev Avramov. Integral ascent of the West Ridge. At the summit on the 20th of April: Hristo Ivanov Prodanov, solo and without oxygen. The route was repeated on the 8th and 9th of May by Ivan Vulchev, Metodi Stefanov Savov, Nikolai Petkov and Kiril Doskov,who then descended along the classic South Col route.

**1984:** Indian expedition led by Darshan Kumar Kullar. Classic Nepalese route. At the summit on the 9th of

*30 left  the 1982 Russian route on the buttress of the Southwest Face* **[A]**. Photo by Keiichi Yamada/Chris Bonington Picture Library

*30 right  In 1983 the American expedition led by J. Morrissey followed a difficult route on the East Face* **[A]**. *In the May of 1988, the British Stephen Venables and two companions opened another demanding route, further to the left, that emerged near the South Col* **[B]**. Photo by Doug Scott

Dorje and Sundare. Two days later the climb was repeated by Pat Morrow, with the Sherpas Pema Dorje and Lhakpa Tsering.

**1982:** the first solo ascent via the South Col on the 27th of December, by the Japanese climber Yasuo Kato, his third ascent of Everest.

**1983:** American expedition led by Gerhard Lenser. Classic Nepalese route. At the summit on the 7th of May: Peter Jamieson, Gerald Roach, David Breashears, Larry Nielson and the Sherpa Ang Rita. The climb was repeated on the 14th of May by Gary Neptune, Jim States and the Sherpa Lhakpa Dorje II.

**1983:** the first ascent of the East Face by an American expedition led by James Morrissey. Carlos Buhler, Kim Momb and Louis Reichardt reached the summit on the 8th of October. The climb was repeated the following day by Jay Cassell, George Lowe and Daniel Reid.

**1983:** Japanese expedition led by Haruichi Kawamura. South Buttress and Southeast Ridge. At the summit on the 8th of October: Haruichi Kawamura and Shomi Suzuki.

May: the Sherpa Phu Dorje. On the 23rd of May the climb was repeated by Miss Bachendri Pal, with Dorje Lhatoo, Sonam Palzor and the Sherpa Ang Dorje (his second ascent of Everest).

**1984:** an Australian group led by Geoffrey Bartram climbed the Great Couloir (Norton Couloir) on the North Face. Tim McCartney-Snape and Greg Mortimer reached the summit on the 3rd of October.

**1984:** Czech expedition led by Frantisek Kele. Ascent via the South Buttress. At the summit on the 15th of October: Jozef Psotka, Zoltan Demjan and the Sherpa Ang Rita (his second ascent of Everest).

**1984:** on the 20th of October, the American Phil Ershler opened a new route from the Northeast Ridge across the North Face at an altitude of 7,300 metres and along the Great Couloir. Ershler was part of a group led by Louis W. Whittaker.

**1985:** Norwegian expedition led by Arne Naess. Classic Nepalese route. Between the 21st and 30th of April 9 climbers and 8 Sherpas reached the summit: Odd Eliassen, Bjorn Myrer-Lund, Pertemba (his third

ascent of Everest), Ang Lhakpa Dorje, Chris Bonington, Dawa Norbu, Arne Naess, Stein Aasheim, Haavard Nesheim, Ralph Hölbakk, Sundare (his fourth ascent to the summit), Ang Rita (his third ascent to the summit), Pema Dorje (his second ascent of Everest), Chowang Rinzing, Richard Bass, David Breashears (his second ascent of Everest), Ang Phurba II.

**1985:** Catalan expedition led by Conrad Blanch. North Col and Northeast Ridge. At the summit on the 28th of August: Toni Sors, Oscar Cadiach and Carles Vallés, with the Sherpas Ang Karma, Shambu Tamang (his second ascent of Everest) and Narayan Shrestha.

**1985:** Japanese expedition led by Kuniaki Yagihara. Classic Nepalese route. At the summit on the 30th of October: Etsuo Akutsu, Satoshi Kimoto, Hideji Nazuka, Teruo Saegusa, Mitsuyoshi Sato, Kuniaki Yagihara and Noboru Yamada (his second ascent of Everest).

**1986:** Canadian expedition led by Jim Elzinga. West Ridge, reached from the Tibetan side. At the summit on the 20th of May: Sharon Wood and Dwayne Congdon.

**1986:** Franco-Swiss expedition led by Pierre Béghin. The Swiss climbers Jean Troillet and Erhard Loretan completed a very rapid climb along the Japanese gully route (with an initial variation) and the Hornbein Couloir, reaching the summit on the 30th of August.

**1987:** South Korean winter expedition led by Hahm Tak-Young. Classic Nepalese route. At the summit on the 22nd of December: Huh Young-ho and the Sherpa Ang Rita (his fourth ascent).

**1988:** Chinese-Japanese-Nepalese expedition. The first traverse of Everest from north to south (North Col – summit – South Col) and vice versa. May 5th: after having climbed the Northeast Ridge the Japanese Noboru Yamada (his third ascent of Chomolungma), the Sherpa Ang Lhakpa Nuru and the Tibetan Tserin Dorje reached the summit. An hour later, via the classic Nepalese route, Ang Phurba II, Ringen Puncog and Da Tsering also reached the summit. At around 13.00 a Japanese TV team arived at the summit via the Northeast Ridge (Susuma Nakamura, Shoji Nakamura and Teruo Saegusa), followed by three more climbers (the Japanese Munehiko Yamamoto, the Chinese Li Zhixin and the Sherpa Lhakpa Sona). Shortly afterwards the first two teams to reach the summit headed down on the opposite sides to complete the traverse. Lastly, on the 10th of May, the Nepalese Sundare (his fifth ascent of Everest) and Padma Bahadur reached the summit by way of the South Col.

**1988:** on the 12th of May the British climber Stephen Venables reached the summit after having opened a new route with two companions (Edward Webster and Robert Anderson) on the East Face.

**1988:** Australian expedition led by Austin Brookes. Classic Nepalese route. At the summit on the 25th of May: Paul Bayne and Patrick Cullinan. The climb was repeated on the 28th of May by John Muir.

**1988:** French expedition led by François Poissonier. Classic Nepalese route. At the summit on the 26th of September: Jean-Marc Boivin, Michel Metzger, Jean-Pierre Frachon, Gérard Vionnet-Fausset, André Georges and the Sherpas Pasang Tsering, Sonam Tsering and Ajiwa.

**1988:** South Korean expedition led by Choi Chang-Min. South Buttress and classic Nepalese route (Southeast Ridge). At the summit on the 26th of September: Kim Chang-Sun, Uh Hong-Gil and the Sherpa Pema Dorje (his third ascent of Everest). The climb was repeated on the 29th of September by Jang Bong-Wan, Chang Byong-Ho and Chung Seung-Kwon. Lastly, Nam Sun-Woo also reached the summit on the 2nd of October.

**1988:** the French climber Marc Batard climbed Everest (without oxygen), along the South Col route, in 22.30 hours from base camp to the summit, exploiting the trails left by the other expeditions operating on the mountain.

**1988:** American expedition led by James Frush. Nepalese route. At the summit on the 29th of September: Stacy Allison and the Sherpa Pasang Gyalzen. On the 2nd of October the climb was repeated by Peggy Luce and Geoffrey Tabin, with the Sherpas Nima Tashi, Phu Dorje and Dawa Tsering.

**1988:** French expedition led by Serge Koenig. Classic Nepalese route. At the summit on the 13th of October: Serge Koenig, Lhakpa Sonam and (probably) Pasang Temba.

*31 top left The Great Couloir route followed by the 1984 Australian expedition [A]. The 1984 Ershler route [B].* Photo by Chris Curry/Hedgehog House

*31 bottom left Two men from the 1988 British expedition about to inaugurate the new East Face route.* Photo by Stephen Venables/ Freestyle Agency

*31 above Canadian expedition led by W. March climbed to the summit via the classic Nepalese route in October 1982.* Photo by Pat Morrow

**1988**: Catalan expedition led by Lluis Belvis. Classic Nepalese route. At the summit on the 14th of October: Nil Bohigas, Jeronimo Lopez and Lluis Giner, with the Sherpas Ang Rita (his fifth ascent of Everest) and Nima Rita.

**1988:** New Zealander expedition led by Rob Hall. Classic Nepalese route. At the summit on the 14th of October: Lydia Bradey (without oxygen).

**1988:** Czech expedition led by Ivan Fiala. Southwest Face. At the summit on the 17th of October: Jozef Just.

**1989:** Yugoslav expedition led by Jovan Poposki. Classic Nepalese route. At the summit on the 10th of May: Stipe Bozic (Croatian), Dimitar Ilijevski (Macedonian) and Viktor Groselj (Slovenian), with the Sherpas Ajiwa and Sonam Tsering (both climbing Everest for the second time).

**1989:** American expedition led by Walt McConnell. Classic Nepalese route. At the summit on the 16th of May: Ricardo Torres (Mexican), with the Sherpas Ang Dannu and Phu Dorje (his second ascent of Everest).

**1989:** American expedition led by Karen Fellerhoff. Classic Nepalese route. At the summit on the 24th

of May: Adrian Burgess (British) and Roddy MacKenzie (Australian), with the Sherpas Ang Lhakpa Nuru (his second ascent of Everest) and Sonam Dendu.

**1989:** Polish expedition led by Eugeniusz Chrobak. West Ridge and Hornbein Couloir. At the summit on the 24th of May: Eugeniusz Chrobak and Andrzej Marciniak.

**1989:** Japanese expedition led by Ken Kanazawa. Classic Nepalese route. At the summit on the 13th of October: Toichiro Mitani, Hiroshi Ohnishi, Atsushi Yamamoto, with the Nepalese Tsering Thebe Lama and Chulin Dorje.

**1989:** South Korean expedition led by Kim In-Tae. South Buttress and Southeast Ridge. At the summit on the 13th of October: Cho Kwang-Je.

**1989:** Mexican expedition led by Carlos Carsolio. Classic Nepalese route. At the summit on the 13th of October: Carlos Carsolio.

**1989:** South Korean expedition led by Lee Suk-Woo. West Ridge. At the summit on the 23rd of October: Chung Sang-Yong, with the Sherpas Nuru Jangbu and Nima Rita (his second ascent of Everest).

**1990:** Nepalese military expedition led by Chitra Badahur Gurung. Classic Nepalese route. At the summit on the 23rd of October: Ang Rita (his sixth ascent of Everest), Ang Kami (his second ascent), Pasang Norbu and Top Bahadur Khatri.

**1990:** international expedition led by Jim Whittaker. North Col and Northeast Ridge. At the summit on the 7th of May: the Americans Robert Link and Steve Gall, the Russian Sergei Arsentiev, the Kazakistani Grigori Lunyakov and the Tibetans Da Cheme and Gyal Bu. The climb was repeated the following day by the Americans Ed Viesturs and Ian Wade, the Ukrainian Mstislav Gorbenko and the Kazakistani Andrei Tselinshchev. Then, on the 9th of May, four more Tibetans climbed to the summit: Gui Sang, Da Qiong, Luo Tse, and Ren Na. Lastly, the following day, the Russians Yekaterina Ivanova, Anatoly Moshnikov and Aleksander Tokarev,the Kazakistani Ervand Ilynski, the American Marc Tucker and the Tibetan Wang-Ja all reached the summit. (Arsentiev, Luniakov, Viesturs and Moshnikov did not use oxygen).

**1990:** American expedition led by Glenn Porzak. Classic Nepalese route. At the summit on the 10th of May: Peter Athans, Glenn Porzak, Dana Coffield, Brent Manning and Michael Browning, with the Sherpas Ang Jangbu, Nima Tashi (his second ascent of Everest) and Dawa Nuru. Andrew Lapkass also reached the summit on the 11th of May.

**1990:** international expedition led by the New Zealander Rob Hall. Classic Nepalese route. At the summit on the 10th of May: New Zealanders Rob Hall, Peter Hillary and Gary Ball, and Belgian Rudy van Snick and the Sherpa

*32 top left* Climbers from the French expedition led by Marc Batard reached the summit of Everest via the classic Nepalese route on the 5th of October 1990. Photo by Pascal Tournaire

*32 bottom left* The French climber Christine Janin, already at an altitude of 8,500 metres, climbs towards the summit of Everest. Photo by Pascal Tournaire

*32 right* The route followed by the 1991 Italian expedition [A]. Photo by Chris Curry/Hedgehog House

Apa. The following day the climb was repeated by the Swedes Mikael Reuterswärd and Oskar Khilborg.

**1990:** the Australian Tim Macartney Snape departed on foot from the Bay of Bengal with two non-climbing friends. Having reached the Everest base camp on the Nepalese side of the mountain he continued along the classic South Col route and reached the summit on the 11th of May without using oxygen.

**1990:** commercial expedition led by the American Hooman Aprin. Classic Nepalese route. At the summit on the 4th of October: Alex Lowe and the Canadian Dan Culver, followed the day after by the expedition leader and Ang Temba. Lastly, on the 7th of October, the climb was repeated by the American Cathy Gibson, the Russian Aleksei Krasnokutsky and the Sherpa Phinjo.

**1990:** French commercial expedition led by Laurence de la Ferrière. Classic Nepalese route. Yves Salino reached the summit on the 4th of October. Three days later Jean-Noël Roche, Bertrand "Zebulon" Roche, Denis Pivot, Alain Desez, the Dutchman René de Bos, and the Sherpas Ang Phurba III and Nima Dorje followed in his footsteps.

**1990:** French expedition led by Marc Batard. Classic Nepalese route. At the summit on the 5th of October: Erik Decamp, Marc Batard (his second ascent), Christine Janin, Pascal Tournaire, and the Sherpas Nawang Thile and Sonam Dendu (his second ascent of Everest). The following day the summit was also reached by the Sherpa Babu Tsering.

**1990:** Japanese-South Korean expedition led by Nobuo Kuwahara and Roh Jong-Baek. Classic Nepalese route. At the summit on the 6th of October: Kim Jee-Soo, Park

Chang-Woo and Bok Jin Young (Koreans), with the Sherpas Dawa Sange and Pemba Dorje.

**1990:** Slovenian expedition led by Tomaz Jamnik. Classic Nepalese route. At the summit on the 10th of May: Andrej Stremfelj (for the second time), his wife Marija, Janez Jeglic and the Sherpa Lhakpa Rita.

**1991:** Sherpa expedition led by Lopsang. Classic Nepalese route. At the summit on the 8th of May: Ang Temba II, Sonam Dendu (for the third time), Apa (his second ascent) and the American Peter Athans.

**1991:** American expedition led by Rick Wilcox. Classic Nepalese route. At the summit on the 15th of May: Mark Richey, Rick Wilcox, Barry Rugo and the Canadian Yves La Forest.

**1991:** American expedition led by Eric Simonson. Classic Tibeten North Col route. At the summit on the 15th of May: Eric Simonson, Bob Sloezen, George Dunn and Andy Politz, with the Sherpas Lhakpa Dorje (for the second time) and Ang Dawa. Two days later the climb was repeated by the New Zealander Mike Perry. Then, on the 21st of May, the New Zealander Mark Whetu and the American Brent Okida also climbed to the summit. The last climber from the expedition to reach the top on the 24th of May was the American Greg Wilson.

**1991:** American expedition led by Robert Link and Ed Viesturs. Classic Nepalese route. Viesturs reached the summit on the 15th of May.

**1991:** Swedish expedition led by Jack Berg. North Face (Japanese route and the Hornbein Couloir ). On the 15th of May the Sherpas Mingma Norbu and Gyalbu reached the summit followed, on the 20th, by Lars Cronlund.

**1991:** an Italian expedition led by Oreste Forno, opened a partially new route along the Great Couloir. The itinerary unfolded to the left of the 1984 Australian route and then tackled directly the difficult rock wall barring the gully at an altitude of 8,400 meters. Battistino Bonali and Leopold Sulovsky reached the summit on the 17th of May.

**1991:** international expedition led by Harry Taylor and Russel Brice. Classic Tibetan North Col route. At the summit on the 22nd of May: the Sherpas Babu Tsering (for the second time) and Chuldin.

**1991:** Japanese expedition led by Muneo Nukita. Classic Tibetan North Col route. At the summit on the 27th of May: Muneo Nikita, Junichi Futagami and the Sherpas Finjo Norbu Nima and Dorje (the latter on the summit of Everest for the second time).

**1991:** Spanish expedition led by Juan-Carlos Gomez. Classic Nepalese route. At the summit on the 6th of October: José Antonio Garcés, Francisco José Pérez, Rafael Vidaurre and Antonio Ubieto.

**1991:** Russian-American expedition led by Volodya Balyberdin. Classic Nepalese route. At the summit on the 7th of October: the Russian Volodia Balyberdin (for the second time) and the Kazakistani Anatoli Boukreev. Then on the 10th of October the Georgian Roman Giutashvili and the American Daniel Mazur also reached the summit.

**1992:** Indian expedition led by Hulam Singh. Classic Nepalese route. On the 10th of May Prem Singh, Sunil Dutt Sharma and Kanhayalal Pokhriyal reached the summit. Two days later the climb was repeated by the Sherpas Lobsang, Sange and Wangchuk, by a woman, Santosh Yadev, and by Mohan Singh Gunjyal.

**1992:** international expedition led by the New Zealander Rob Hall. Classic Nepalese route. The summit was reached on the 12th of May by the New Zealanders Rob Hall (his second ascent of Everest), Gary Ball (his second ascent) and Guy Cotter, the Americans Ned Gillette, Douglas Mantle and Randall Danta, the Hong Kong Chinese Cham Yick-Kai, the Israeli Doron Erel, the Belgian Ingrid Baeyens and the Sherpas Sonam Tsering (for third time), Ang Dorje II, Tashi Tsering, Apa (his third ascent of Everest) and Ang Dawa (his second ascent).

**1992:** Dutch expedition led by Ronald Naar. Classic Nepalese route. At the summit on the 12th of May: Ronald Naar, Edmond Öfner and the Sherpas Dawa Tashi and Nima Temba.

**1992:** Russian expedition led by Vyacheslav Volkov. Classic Nepalese route. At the summit on the 12th of May: Aleksandr Gerasimov, Andrei Volkov, Ivan Dusharin and Ilia Sabelnikov. On the 14th of May the climb was repeated by Sergei Penzov, Vladimir Zakharov, Yevgeni Vinogradsky and Fiodor Konyukhov.

**1992:** American expedition led by Todd Burleson. Classic Nepalese route. The summit was reached on the 12th of May by Skip Horner, Louis Bowen and Vernon Tejas, with the Sherpas Dawa Temba and Ang Gyalzen. Three days later the climb was repeated by

Peter Athans, Todd Burleson, Hugh Morton, the Briton Keith Kerr and the Sherpas Lhakpa Rita (his second ascent), Man Bahadur Tamang and Dorje.

**1992:** Chilean expedition led by Rodrigo Jordan. East Face as far as the South Col and then classic Nepalese route. At the summit on the 15th of May: Cristian-Garcia Huidobro, Rodrigo Jordan and Juan-Sebastian Montes.

**1992:** Spanish expedition led by Francisco Soria. South Buttress. The summit was reached on the 15th of May by Francisco Gan, Alfonso Juez and Ramon Portilla with the Sherpas Lhakpa Nuru and Pemba Norbu II.

**1992:** Chilean expedition led by Mauricio Purto. Classic Nepalese route. The summit was reached on the 15th of May by Mauricio Purto and the Sherpas Ang Rita (his seventh ascent) and Ang Phuri.

**1992:** international expedition led by the Czech Miroslav Smid. Classic Nepalese route. The summit was reached on the 15th of May by the Briton Jonathan Pratt.

**1992:** Basque expedition led by Pedro Tous. Classic Nepalese route. The summit was reached on the 25th of September by Pitxi Eguillor, Patxi Fernández, Alberto Iñurrategi, Félix Iñurrategi. The ascent was repeated on the 1st of October by Josu Bereziartua and, two days later, by Mikel Repáraz, Pedro Tous and Juan Tomás.

**1992:** Italian expedition led by Agostino Da Polenza. Classic Nepalese route. At the summit on the 28th of September: Giuseppe Petigax, Lorenzo Mazzoleni, Mario Panzeri, the Frenchman Pierre Royerand and the Sherpa Lhakpa Nuru (his second ascent). The following day the climb was repeated by Oswald Santin, Abele Blanc, Giampietro Verza and the Frenchman Benoît Chamoux.

**1992:** international expedition led by the Frenchman Bernard Muller. Classic Nepalese route. On the 1st of October the summit was reached by the Luxembourger Eugène Berger.

**1992:** international expedition led by the German Ralf Dujmovits. Classic Nepalese route. The summit was reached on the 4th of October by Dujmovits and the Sherpa Sonam Tsering (his fourth ascent of Everest).

**1992:** international expedition led by the Frenchman Michel Vincent. Classic Nepalese route. The summit was reached on the 7th of October by Vincent, followed two days later by the American Scott Darsney.

**1992:** international expedition led by the American Wally Berg. Classic Nepalese route. At the summit on the 9th of October: Berg, the Peruvian Augusto Ortega and the Mexican Alfonso de la Parra, along with the Sherpas Apa (his fourth ascent) and Pasang Kami.

**1992:** French expedition led by Michel Pellé. At the summit on the 9th of October: Pellé, Philippe Grenier, Thierry Defrance, Alain Russey and Pierre Aubertin.

**1993:** Korean expedition led by Oh in-Hwan. An unplanned traverse from North to South. After reaching the peak in the afternoon of the 13th of April, following the classic North Col route, Heo Young-Ho and the

*33 top* In the autumn of 1992 the Italian EV-K²-CNR expedition measured the height of Everest.
Photo by Mountain Equipe Archive

*33 bottom right* The North Face of Everest has been the target of innumerable expeditions during the 1990s.
Photo by Galen Rowell

Sherpa Ngati preferred to descend on the Nepalese side due to bad weather.

**1993:** Sherpa expedition led by the Sherpa Pasang Lhamu. Classic Nepalese route. The summit was reached on the 22nd of April by: Pasang Lhamu, Sonam Tsering, Dawa Tashi, Lakpha Nuru, Pemba Nuru and Nawang Thile.

**1993:** Sino-Taiwanese expedition led by the Chinese climber Zebg Shu-sheng. Classic Tibetan North Col route. The summit of Everest was gained on the 5th of May by the Chinese Chhimi, Gyatso, Khetsun, Phubu and Wag Yong-Feng and by the Taiwanese Wu Chin-Hsiung.

**1993:** international expedition led by the American Todd Burleson. Classic Nepalese route. At the summit on the 10th of May: the Americans Alex Lowe, John Helenek, John Dufficy, Wally Berg and the Canadian Michael Sutton, with the Sherpas Apa, Dawa Nuru, and Chuldin Temba.

**1993:** South Korean women's expedition led by Ji Hyun-Ok. Classic Nepalese route. At the summit on the 10th of May: Hyun-Ok and Choi Oh-Soon, with the Sherpas Ang Dawa, Ang Tsering, Sona Dendu and Rinzin.

**1993:** international expedition led by the Sherpa Tashi Tenzing. Classic Nepalese route. On the 10th of May the summit was reached by the Australian Michael Groom and the Indian Lbsang Tsgering Buthia.

**1993:** British expedition led by John Barry. Classic Nepalese route. Harry Taylor reached the summit on the 10th of May. On the 17th, the climb was repeated by Rebecca Stephens and the Sherpas Ang Pasang and Kami Tsering.

**1993:** Indian women's expedition led by Bachendri Pal. Classic Nepalese route. At the summit on the 10th of May:

Dickey Dolma, Santosh Yadav, Kunga Bhutia, Baldev Kunwer, and the Sherpas Ongda Chiring, Na Temba and Kosang Dorje. On the 16th of May the climb was repeated by Radha Devi Thakur, Rajiv Sharma, Deepu Sharma, Savita Martolia, Norbu Dolma, Suman Kutyal and the Sherpas Nima Dorje, Tenzing, Lobsang Jangbu, Nga Temba.

**1993:** American expedition led by Michael Sinclair. Classic Nepalese route. At the summit on the 10th of May: Mary (Dolly) Lefever, Mark Selland, Charles Armatys, and the Sherpas Pema Temba and Moti Lal Gurung. On the 16th of May Michael Sinclair, Mark Rabold and the Sherpas Phinzo, Dorje and Durga Tamang also arrived at the summit.

**1993:** international expedition led by Rob Hall. Classic Nepalese route. At the summit on the 10th of May: the Finn Veikka Gustaffson, the New Zealanders Jan Arnold, Rob Hall and Jonathan Gluckman, and the Sherpas Ang Chumbi, Ang Dorje and Nuru.

**1993:** on the 10th of May the Lithuanian Vladas Vitkauskas reached the summit via the South Col.

**1993:** Russian expedition led by Aleksandr Volgin. Following an attempt on the West Ridge, the group climbed along the classis Nepalese route. On the 10th of May Aleksei Muraviov reached the summit, followed by Vladimir Janochkin (on the 15th), Vladimir Bashkirov (the 16th) and Vladimir Koroteyev (the 17th of May).

**1993:** Catalan expedition led by Lluis Belvis. Classic Nepalese route. At the summit on the 16th of May: Josep Pujante and the Sherpa Ang Phurba. The climb was repeated the following day by Oscar Cadiach.

**1993:** Basque expedition led by Josu Feijoo. Classic Nepalese route. At the summit on the 16th of May: Joxe Maria Oñate, Alberto Zerain, José Ramon Aguirre, and the Sherpas Jongbu and Ang Rita (his eighth ascent of Everest!).

**1993:** American expedition led by Keith Brown. Classic Nepalese route. Brown and Jan Harris reached the summit on the 16th of May.

**1993:** South Korean expedition led by Lee Jong-Ryang. An attempt on the Southwest face and an ascent along the classic Nepalese route. At the summit on the 16th of May: Park Young-Seok, An Jin-Seob, Kim Tae-Kon, and the Sherpa Kaji.

**1993:** Irish expedition led by Dawson Stelfox. Classic Tibetan route via the North Col. Stelfox reached the summit on the 27th of May.

**1993:** South Korean expedition led by Lim Hyung-Chil. Classic Tibetan North Col route. At the summit on the 6th of October: Park Huyn-Jae and the Sherpa Pa Nuru.

**1993:** French military expedition led by Alain Estève. Classic Nepalese route. At the summit on the 6th of October: François Bernard, Antoine Cayrol, Eric Gramond, and the Sherpas Gyalbu and Dawa Tashi. The climb was repeated three days later by Estève, Hubert Giot and the Sherpas Nuru and Gombu.

**1993:** Basque expedition led by Juan Oiarzabal. South Buttress. On the 7th of October, Oiarzabal and the Sherpa Ongda Chiring reached the summit.

**1993:** British expedition led by Stephen Bell. Classic Nepalese route. At the sumit on the 7th of October: Bell, Ginette Harrison, Graham Hoyland, Scott McIver, the Spanish climber Ramon Blanco, the American Gary Pfisterer and the Sherpas Na Temba, Pasang Kamo and Dorje. Two days later the climb was repeated by Martin Barnicott and David Hempleman-Adams, the American

Lee Nobbman and the Sherpas Tenzing, Nga Tembva, Lhakpa Gelu and Ang Pasang.

**1993:** international commercial expedition led by the Briton Jonathan Tinker. Classic Tibetan North Col route. At the summit on the 9th of October: the Pole Maciej Berbeka and the Sherpa Lhakpa Nuru, followed, the day after, by Tinker and the Sherpa Babu Tsering.

**1993:** Japanese expedition led by Kuniaki Yagihara, Yoshio Ogata and Hideji Nazuka. First winter ascent of the Southwest Face. After just three weeks in the area, Hideji Nazuka and Fumiaki Goto reached the summit on the 18th of December. two days later the climb was repeated by Osamu Tanabe and Sinsuke Exuka, followed a further two days later by Yoshio Ogata and Ryushi Hoshino.

**1994:** Japanese expedition led by Mitsuyoshi Hongo. South Buttress. At the summit on the 8th of May Kiyohiko Suzuki, Wataru Atsuta, and the Sherpas Nima Dorje and Dawa Tsering, Na Temba and Lhakpa Nuru. On the 13th of May the climb was repeated by Tomiyasu Ishikawa and the Sherpas Nima Tema, Dawa Tashi and Pasang Tsering.

**1994:** international commercial expedition led by the New Zealander Rob Hall and the American Ed Viesturs. Classic Nepalese route. At the summit on the 9th of May: Hall (his fourth ascent of Everest), Viesturs (for the third time), the Americans Hall Wendel, David Keaton and David Taylor, the Germans Hellmut Seitzl and Ekkert Gundelbach, the Norwegian Erling Kagge, and the Sherpas Ang Dorje, Nima Norbu and Norbu.

**1994:** American expedition led by Steven Goryl. Classic Nepalese route. At the summit on the 13th of May: Rob Hess, Scott Fischer, Brent Bishop, and the Sherpas Lobsang Sangbu and Sonam Dindu. Goryl also reached the summit on the 13th.

**1994:** commerical expedition led by the American Todd Burleson. Classic Nepalese route. The summit was reached on the 13th of May by the Americans Burleson, Robert Cedergreen, Paul Morrow and Peter Athans, the Pole Ryszard Pawlowski, Tamang Man Bahadur, and the Sherpas Lhakpa Rita, Chuwang Nima, Kami Rita and Dorje.

**1994:** international commercial expedition led by the American Eric Simonson. Classic Tibetan North Col route. Dave Hahan reached the summit on the 19th of May. He was followed on the 26th by Michael Rheinberger and Mark Whetu (his second ascent along the same route), and on the 31st by Bob Sloezen (his second ascent of Everest).

**1994:** Japanese expedition. Classic Nepalese route. At the summit on the 10th of October: Muneo Nukita and the Sherpas Apa, Chuwang Nima and Dawa.

**1994:** international expedition led by Simon Currin. The summit was reached on the 11th of October by the Britons Charlie Hornsby and Roddy Kirkwood and the Sherpas Dorje and Dawa Temba.

**1995:** commercial expedition led by Rob Hall. Classic Nepalese route. The Sherpa Lobsang Jangbu reached the summit on the 7th of May.

**1995:** Russian expedition led by Kazbek Khamitsayev. Classic Tibetan North Col route. On the 10th of May three climbers reached the summit (including Vladimir Shataev). Followed three days later by the expedition leader, three companions (including Sergei Bogomolov), and the Sherpa Ang Rita (his ninth ascent of Everest)

**1995:** Japanese expedition led by Tadeo Kanzaki and Kiyoshi Furuno. First integral ascent of the Northeast Ridge. The route was equipped with the aid of 23 Sherpas and 4,000 meters of fixed ropes. The lead group (Furuno and Shigeki Imoto, with the Sherpas Lhakpa Nuru, Dawa Tsering, Nima Dorje and Pasang Kami) reached the summit on the 11th of May. For Lhakpa Nuru this was the sixth ascent Everest, and the fifth for Nima Dorje.

**1995:** Italo-Polish expedition led by Marco Bianchi. Classic Tibetan North Col route. On the 12th of May Piotr Pustelnik reached the summit with Ryszard Pawlowski (both used oxygen).
The latter was a Polish climber from Henry Todd's commercial expedition. Bianchi and Christian Kuntner reached the summit on the 13th of May without using oxygen.

**1995:** international commercial expedition led by Russel Brice. Classic Tibetan North Col route. The Briton Alison Hargreaves reached the summit without oxygen on the 13th of May. Before her, in 1988, Everest had been scaled without oxygen by another woman climber, the New Zealander Lydia Bradey, but she lacked a permit for her ascent via the South Col. On the 17th of May the Romanian Constantin Lacatusu reached the summit, followed on the 26th by the Australian Greg Child and two Sherpas.

**1995:** international commercial expedition led by John Tinker. Classic Tibetan North Col route. Between the 14 and the 27th of May, nine climbers reached the summit together with the Sherpas. Among the latter was Babu Tsering (five ascents without oxygen and two in the same month, on the 14th and the 26th of May!).

**1995:** international commercial expedition led by Henry Todd. Classic Tibetan North Col route. Between the 12th and the 23rd of May, eight climbers reached the summit: Ryszard Pawlowski (Polish), Anatoli Boukreev (Kazakistani, his second ascent of Everest), Nikoli Sitnikov (Russian), Graham Ratcliffe (English), Michael Jorgenson (Danish), Craig Jones (Welsh), Mozart Catao and Waldemar Niclevicz (Brazilian).

**1995:** Taiwanese expedition. Classic Tibetan North Col route. Chiang Hsiu-Chen, a woman, reached the summit on the 12th of May.

**1995:** Latvian expedition led by the Italian Reinhard Patscheider. Classic Tibetan North Col route Very early on the 14th of May Patscheider reached the summit of Everest, taking just 21 hours from 6,450 meters.

On the same day Teodors Kirsis and Imants Zauls also reached the summit.

**1995:** American expedition. Classic Tibetan North Col route. At the summit on the 14th of May: the Australian George Mallory (grandson of the celebrated British Everest pioneer), Jeff Hall, Jim Litch, Dan Aguilar and the Sherpas Chirring, Kaji and Wongchu. The climb was repeated on the 16th by Colin Linch, Jay Budnick, Steve Reneker, Kurt Wedberg, and the Sherpas Phinjo and Jangbu.

**1995:** American expedition. Classic Nepalese route. At the summit on the 15th of May: the American Brad Bull, the Argentinian Tommy Heinrich, and three Sherpas.

**1995:** two independent South Korean expeditions joined forces to reach the summit. Classic Tibetan North Col route. Two climbers and three Sherpas reached the summit on the 14th of October.

**1995:** South Korean expedition led by Cho Hyung-Kyu. Southwest Face, British 1975 route. At the summit on the 14th of October: Park Jung-Heon, Kim Young-Tae, and the Sherpas Kipa and Dawa Tamang.

**Note:** *In 1996, there were 87 reported successful ascents of Everest (a few of the more notable are listed below). This brings to over 800 the total number of ascents to the roof of the world; this total represents the achievement of around 660 climbers (since quite a number of individuals have made more than one ascent). In contrast to these triumphs, 143 climbers had lost their lives on the slopes of the mountain (through the end of May 1996)*

**1996:** international commercial expedition led by New Zealander Rob Hall. On the summit on May 10th: Hall, Andy Harris, Michael Groom, Doug Hansen, Jon Krakauer, and Yasuko Namba (oldest woman, at 47, to make the ascent) and Sherpa Ang Dorje.

**1996:** international commercial expedition led by Scott Fischer. On the summit on May 10th: Scott Fischer, Neal Beidleman, Anatoli Boukreev, Lene Gammelgaard (first Danish woman to summit), Charlotte Fox, Tim Madsen, Sandy Hill Pittman, Martin Adams, and Klev Schoening and Sherpas Logsang Jangbu, Tashi Tsering.

**1996:** Taiwanese expedition. On the summit on May 10th: Makalu Gau and Sherpas Nima Gombu and Mingma Tsering.

**1996:** Russian expedition charts a new route following a difficult rock and snow couloir between the North and Northeast Ridges. On the summit on May 20th: Petr Kouznetsov, Valeri Kohanov, and Grigori Semikolenkov.

**1996:** Italian expedition. Very fast ascent (17 hours) via the North Col route by Hans Kammerlander, who reached the summit on May 24rd and then descended on skis.

**1996:** first South African expedition. On the summit on May 25th: Ian Woodall, Cathy O'Dowd, and Bruce Herrod and three unnamed Sherpas.

*34  Ever since the pioneer days, climbing expeditions have pitched high altitude camps at the North Col.
Photo by René Robert/Freestyle Agency*

*35 top  The integral North-east Ridge route followed by the 1995 Japanese expedition* **[A]**.
*Photo by Chris Curry/Hedgehog House*

*35 bottom  In May 1995, Marco Bianchi and Christian Kuntner completed the classic Tibetan route without using oxygen. At the bottom can be seen the ritual flags carried to the summit by the men of the Italian expedition.
Photo by Marco Bianchi*

*36 top  This map, dating back to around 1880, shows the results of the work of the Grand Trigonometrical Survey of the Indian peninsula. During the survey the British officers explored in all directions and circa 1830 came within sight of the Himalayas. The first measurements of the Himalayan peaks, however, did not begin until 1847.*
Photo: Geographical Society

INDEX CHART
TO THE
GREAT TRIGONOMETRICAL SURVEY
OF
INDIA

SHOWING COLONEL LAMBTONS NET WORK OF TRIANGULATION IN SOUTHERN INDIA,
THE MERIDIONAL AND LONGITUDINAL CHAINS OF PRINCIPAL TRIANGLES.
THE BASE LINES MEASURED WITH THE COLBY APPARATUS.
THE LINES OF THE SPIRIT LEVELLING OPERATIONS.
THE ASTRONOMICAL PENDULUM & TIDAL STATIONS.
THE LONGITUDINAL ARCS.
AND THE SECONDARY TRIANGULATION TO FIX THE PEAKS OF
THE HIMALAYAN & THE SOOLIMANI RANGES,
AND THE POSITIONS OF BANGKOK AND KANDAHAR.
Completed to 1st October 1882.
*Enlarged by Photo-Zincography at the Ordnance Survey Office, Southampton, 1885.*

# THE INVENTION OF EVEREST

We are in the year 1852, at the headquarters of the Grand Trigonometrical Survey of India at Dehra Dun, 140 kilometers north-northeast of Delhi. Radhanath Sikdhar, the head of the Computing Office, bursts into the office of the Superintendent General, Sir Andrew Waugh, with some news they had been expecting for months. "Sir, I have discovered the highest mountain in the world!" The legend of Everest began at that moment.

In point of fact, the history books divide the credit for the "discovery" between Sikdhar and Michael Hennessy, Waugh's young assistant. However, within the framework of the general scope of the issue, the question that day appeared quite irrelevant. Even more so because the entire Survey staff had been working for some time on the measurement of the Himalayan peaks, and the final figures announced by the computing chief were in reality the result of long collective calculations. In the history of Himalayism, the event was an important date for another reason. The same fate that had befallen Mont Blanc some decades before now befell Everest. Basically speaking, before it could be climbed, the Himalayan colossus had to be literally "invented"

*36 bottom  Sir George Everest, portrayed here sitting in his study, was the Superintendent General of the Survey of India from 1830 to 1843 as well as one of the pioneers of cartographic surveying on the Indian subcontinent.*
Photo: Royal Geographical Society

within an imaginary framework, and then "discovered" by using a series of complex trigonometric calculations, which were essential to extract and isolate the mighty outline of Peak XV from the chaos of the surrounding peaks.

In reality the lengthy process which led to the "discovery" of Everest started at least fifty years before. It is, however, difficult to trace precisely its origin, because we also have to knot together different stories and interweave events which are scattered and sometimes distant in space and time.

By the beginning of the nineteenth century, about a hundred and fifty years after the establishment of the first English agencies at Madras, Bombay and Calcutta, India was almost totally under British control. But the Raj, the British Empire, needed to consolidate its power, keeping an eye on the international chessboard, with special attention to Russian attempts at expansion in central Asia—above all in the Hindu Kush, the Pamir and Tibet—which were still unknown and uncharted. It was no coincidence that right in the center of the continent, the imperialist greed of the two

providing the British colony with suitable cartographical support began later, at the turn of the next century, with the founding of the Grand Trigonometrical Survey.

In 1823 Colonel George Everest came onto the stage, as Superintendent of the Indian Trigonometrical Survey, and for many years, till 1843, he worked tirelessly on an ambitious project: a grid survey of the whole Raj. But his aims also included the mathematical calculation of the great meridian arc which rises from Cape Comorin at the southern end of the Indian peninsula, and crosses the Himalayan chain. The measurement of the latter was to make it possible to determine the mathematical geoid (the theoretical ideal sphere) on which to calculate the heights of the mountains.

During their surveys the officials moved in almost all directions, and in the 1830s came within sight of the Himalayas. The English had for some time suspected that the orographic nodes of the great mountain chain contained some of the highest mountains on Earth. Already at the beginning of the nineteenth century, Colebrooke and Webb, the explorers of the Ganges and its

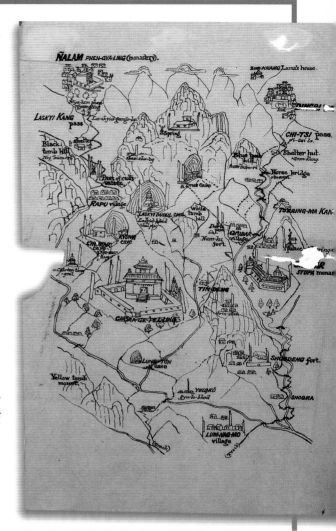

powers was shortly afterwards to start that spy war which in Great Britain took the name of the Great Game, and which the Russians, more picturesquely, were to call the Shadow Tournament.

It is clear that in such a setting the British stationed in India felt the need to have an in-depth knowledge of—and to properly control—the territory of the British Raj and bordering regions. The first triangulations in Indian territory date back to 1764 and were carried out in the Ganges Valley, but the ambitious plan of

sources, spoke of very high mountains, some over five miles in height, higher than any peaks in the Andes. But for the moment the figures were still approximate. To find out more, they had to pinpoint the various peaks exactly on the map and, above all, give their exact elevations. There were many hurdles to overcome, because Tibet, Nepal, China, Sikkim and Bhutan barred the way to the topographers. The British were consequently obliged to carry out their measurements from trigonometrical stations quite distant from the actual Himalayan chain.

*37 top  This rather vague topographical sketch constitutes one of the first timid attempts to represent on paper the Himalayan valleys located beyond the borders of the British Raj.*
Photo: Royal Geographical Society

*37 bottom  Sir George Everest and one of his assistants supervising the construction of a survey station. This drawing with its naive and even humorous aspects was executed by the explorer Godfrey Thomas Vigne and is dated 1834.*
Photo: Royal Geographical Society

The first detailed surveys of the Himalayan peaks by the Survey of India began in 1847, on the initiative of the new Superintendent, Colonel Andrew Waugh. In those years, the trigonometrical campaigns were complicated and laborious, because the surveyors could study the peaks only from great distances. Being denied access, in fact, obliged the British military to place their measuring instruments as far as 250 kilometers from the mountains.

It was hard work in those conditions, even more because, due to the monsoons, the surveying teams could count on good visibility only from October to December. But this was not all: to obtain reliable data, the teams studying the Himalayas were forced to use particularly powerful theodolites, of enormous size and all very heavy; so heavy that it took a dozen men to transport one single piece of equipment.

In the autumn of 1847, Waugh was dealing with the measurement of Kangchenjunga, until then considered the highest mountain in the world. Behind the Himalayan giant, however, the Survey Superintendent observed with interest another icy peak which apparently was even higher: in topographic circles it was soon baptized with the name of "Peak B." It was extremely difficult, at that moment, to hazard predictions, but from that sighting arose the first doubts about Kangchenjunga. Waugh decided to

pursue the question and increased observations from other trigonometrical stations, which were nearer the Himalayan chain. His officers succeeded in advancing to within 170 kilometers of the mountains, and invariably—though bearing in mind the possibility of errors—all the measurements of "Peak B" indicated a height which was decidedly above that of Kangchenjunga. Subsequently the results of the various surveys were re-examined in the offices at Dehra Dun. The process of calculation lasted for a few years, because each datum obtained by the topographers had to be stripped of the effects of the refraction of light and the excessive distance of the peak from the survey stations. In the meantime, Michael Hennessy, one of Colonel Waugh's assistants, invented a new naming system for the Himalayan mountains, identifying the most important peaks with Roman numerals. Kangchenjunga was thus

renamed Peak IX, and Peak B became Peak XV. Lastly, after much effort, came the final results which were made official only in 1856: 28,156 feet (8,581.9 meters), Peak IX and 29,002 feet (8,839.8 meters), Peak XV. Very prudently, Waugh declared that the latter might prove to be the highest mountain in the world.

But the discovery was not yet complete. For a proper baptism, a number is not enough. The Himalayan giant needed a more dignified toponym. In Nepal no one had ever assigned a specific name to Peak XV, apart from that of the mountain chain which closes the Khumbu Valley. In Tibet, on the other hand, the inhabitants of the lands north of the Himalayas call the gigantic snowy peak, which stands out imposingly against the horizon, Chomolungma (or Tschoumon-Lanckma, the Goddess Mother of the World). But for the British, the local place names were not enough. Waugh therefore suggested calling the Survey's discovery after his predecessor, Sir George Everest, and some years later, in 1865, the Royal Geographical Society officially accepted the proposal.

But the topographers' calculations were only the first step in drawing closer to the mountain. In reality, at the end of the nineteenth century, very little was known about Everest. Until then the British had observed the Himalayan chain as from their balcony, so to speak. They had succeeded in identifying the highest peaks through the lenses of their theodolites, but knew nothing of what stretched beyond the northern limits of the British colony. Beyond a certain latitude, for Westerners there was only a geographic vacuum. The topographic maps of the British Raj fade into uncertainty, betraying stretches of pure fantasy, or show large white patches. In short, the great mountains of central Asia still belonged to the world of the imagination, or at least the undefined, and the representation of the Himalayan world was only an interweaving of hypotheses. In some aspects they seem to have gone back in time, to the period when explorers started off in search of new lands and imaginary regions. In any case, the last years of the nineteenth century were to bring discoveries and surprises.

It is difficult for a cartographer to imagine anything more exciting than the detailed drafting of a geographical map after years of vain research and attempts ending in failure. In the case of the Himalayas, however, for a certain period the topographers' work proceeded with an exasperating slowness. The road northwards was barred to the British stationed in India with no chance of appeal. In the last half of the nineteenth century, there was absolutely no way of crossing the border which gave access to the great mountains. And so, for twenty years after 1865, those in charge of the Survey carried out secret strategies and operating plans to explore the forbidden territories. A group of Indians, belonging to different races, who had the somatic features of the inhabitants of the two sides of the Himalayas, were submitted to long training by J.T.

Walker and T.G. Montgomerie. The idea was to create a small nucleus of secret agents, able to penetrate beyond the frontier without being recognized—somewhat as William Moorcroft and Hyder Young Hearsey had done in 1812, when disguised as fakirs, they had set off from Bengal, crossed the Himalayas and reached the Tibetan high plateau. Dressed as pilgrims or merchants, the Survey's pundit explorers had been trained to use the sextant and had learned to assess altitudes according to the boiling point of water. They also knew how to take bearings by the stars and to measure the distances they covered by counting their paces, all of standard length, with the help of a Buddhist rosary on which 100 beads were threaded (instead of the 108 traditionally used). Each topographic instrument, each travel note in their possession had to be carefully hidden: in the

# PUNDITS, EXPLORERS, MOUNTAINEERS

hollow of a walking stick, in prayer cylinders, in some amulet. But just the same it was not easy and the slightest mistake could unmask them— even the different number of prayer beads. Furthermore, the little states in the shelter of the mountains lived on the defensive, and it was not easy for the false pilgrims to pass unnoticed. A thousand watchful eyes followed the travelers, ready to seize on their slightest slip. In any case the pundits stubbornly moved around for years at the foot of the great chain of the Himalayas and the Karakoram, and visited regions of which little was known. Some traveled to the upper valleys of Nepal, others entered Tibet, some approached the Hindu Kush and the Pamir. The best known were called Nain, Mani, Kishen and Kalian Singh, Kintup, Hari Ram, Ata Muhammad, Abdul Subhan, but for reasons of secrecy they only used two initials, and never their own names. Some of them came back to base after years of absence, others were robbed and taken prisoner, and there were some who literally disappeared into thin air. Nain Singh succeeded in reaching Lhasa; Hari Ram, the legendary "M.H.," set off from Darjeeling, crossed Nepal and reached Shigatse in southeast Tibet,

exploring the high mountain massifs around Everest.

Their observations, at times vague but often incredibly accurate, were to be invaluable for the Survey cartographers. Interwoven with the tales of ancient travelers—from de Andrade to de Azevedo, Beligatti da Macerata and Desideri da Pistoia—they helped to provide knowledge on unknown lands and were a primary source of information in drafting the first maps of those remote areas of Asia.

But there were not only the paths of secrecy: every now and then some explorer managed to get a glimpse of Everest in an official manner, without having to overcome too much red tape. Travelers of the 1830s visited Ladakh, Garhwal, Kashmir and Baltistan, and at the end of the following decade Joseph Hooker wandered among the mountains of Sikkim. Ten years later the brothers Adolf, Hermann and Robert Schlagintweit, some of the first explorers to become familiar with ice and rock, searched, in the service of the Survey, many corners of the Karakoram and Himalayas (in 1855 they reached an altitude of 6,785 meters on Abi Gamin, in the Garhwal

*41 top Tom George Longstaff (1875-1964), a great Alpine climber and explorer, was extremely active in the Himalayas. In 1922 he took part in the second British expedition to Everest as a technical advisor. He was President of the Alpine Club from 1947 to 1949.* Photo: Royal Geographical Society

*41 bottom William Martin Conway, a London art critic, writer and explorer (1865-1937), was one of the great Himalayan pioneers. For many years, his 1892 venture into the Karakoram was regarded as a model expedition.* Photo: Royal Geographical Society

region). And shortly afterwards, Henry Haversham Godwin Austen, a Survey official, partially crossed the Baltoro Glacier. With the dawn of the 1880s, exploration recorded a further boost. In 1882-83, the British Alpine climber, W.W. Graham, accompanied by Swiss guides, including Joseph Imboden, went to Garhwal and Sikkim (where he visited the Kangchenjunga region) with the declared aim of carrying out a climbing campaign.

Not much later, British penetration among the great Asian mountains became even more marked. In 1887, Colonel Francis Younghusband, starting out from Sinkiang, crossed the Karakoram by climbing the Mustagh Pass and re-entered British India. In 1892, William Martin Conway pushed on into the heart of the Karakoram with a small climbing expedition. It was truly the beginning of a new epoch, which re-echoes with legendary names of explorers and climbers, like Tom George Longstaff, William Douglas Freshfield, Charles Granville Bruce, John Norman Collie, William Martin Conway and many others. Within a few seasons, explorations and climbs multiplied at a dizzying speed. And a new age began for Himalayan mountaineering.

*40 left William Douglas Freshfield (1845-1934), one of the greatest mountain explorers of all time, completed climbs throughout the world. He was particularly active in the Caucasus and in 1899 he completed a full circle around Kangchenjunga. From 1893 to 1895 he was President of the Alpine Club.* Photo: Royal Geographical Society

*40-41 This unusual panoramic photograph was taken from Sandakphu as noted in the bottom left corner. It shows in the distance the Himalayan range and the Everest complex.* Photo:The British Library

The measuring of Everest, as we have said, marks the beginning of our story. But ultimately the "discovery" of 1852 constituted only a small breach in the wall of mystery surrounding the vast Himalayan chain, the longest in the world, 2,500 kilometers from west to east. And so for many years Earth's highest summit remained no more than a geographical curiosity. Despite the penetration of Nepal and Tibet by the pundits, the idea of climbing Everest was still far from taking shape. In the mid-nineteenth century, mountaineering was still in its infancy, although the foundation of Alpine climbing—the ascent of Mont Blanc—had already taken place some decades before. We just need to glance at any historical handbook to realise this: the major summits in the Alps were not to be scaled until a few years hence, and the Matterhorn, the mountain symbol of Alpine climbing, was to fall only in 1865. The "roof of the world" was too high and too far away to disturb the sleep of mountaineers. The English explorer Sir Francis Younghusband, in one of his books published in London in 1936—*Everest, the Challenge*—on the subject of his famous crossing of

the Karakoram, confesses, "Certainly, the idea never entered my mind as I first travelled amongst the greater Himalayan peaks in 1887." And he adds, "Two years before, I had spoken with an officer of the Survey of India about Graham's reported ascent to about 24,000 feet on Kabru, and he had assured me that Graham must have mistaken his peak, for no man could go so high: 22,000 was the limit." If the truth be known, already in 1885 the writer-climber Clinton Dent had said in one of his books that he was sure Everest could be climbed by man. But generally speaking, at that time, a climbing project at very high altitudes was truly futuristic. Himalayan climbing had to first make a long series of gradual steps. With the passing of the years, however, the call of the heights made itself felt. Martin Conway, who in 1902 was to become President of the Alpine Club, was one of the first not to set himself limits. In 1891 he asked Younghusband's advice: he wanted to attempt a Himalayan summit of 25,000 feet (about 7,600 metres) and only one year later he made an attempt on K2. Three years later Albert Frederick Mummery, considered the founder of modern Alpine climbing, attacked Nanga Parbat (8,125 meters). Twelve years afterwards the first Himalayan "7000" fell; Trisul (7,120 meters) in the Garhwal region, was climbed by Longstaff, with the brothers Alexis and Henri Brocherel and a Gurkha. In 1909 the Italian Duke of the Abruzzi attempted K2 and climbed to 7,489 metres on Chogolisa: a record.

Slowly, climbers began to turn their heads more boldly towards the highest peaks in the Himalayas. In 1911, Alexander Mitchell Kellas climbed Pahunhuri (7,128 meters) in Sikkim. In 1913, Mario Piacenza with some companions scaled Kun. Lastly, between 1913 and 1914, Filippo De Filippi, at the head of a great scientific expedition, crossed Kashmir, Baltistan, and Ladakh, touched Kun Lun and reached Chinese Turkestan (Sinkiang).

But there was someone who had been secretly thinking about the "top of the world" for some years. In 1899, on planning an official visit to Nepal, Lord Curzon, the Viceroy of India, suggested to Douglas Freshfield, the first President of the Alpine Club and head of the Royal Geographical Society, that he should try the road to Everest. He himself would officially ask for access for a British expedition in Nepal. But everything ended at the level of hypothesis. In the meantime, not long afterwards, the question of Tibet became pressing. A possible Russian occupation of the great high plateau north of the Himalayas would constitute a huge threat for

# *T*HE GENESIS OF AN IDEA

*42 top  Colonel Francis Edward Younghusband and a group of British officers posing for the photographer at Phari Dzong during a military mission to Tibet in January 1904.*
Photo: Royal Geographical Society

*42 bottom  The British expedition to Tibet led by Colonel Younghusband spent the winter months camped in the Chumbi Valley. The intense cold, in fact, made the Tibetan highlands inaccessible.*
Photo: Royal Geographical Society

*43 top  The British mission to Tibet of 1903-1904 produced, among other things, interesting photographic documentation of what was still virtually unknown territory. In this photo Younghusband and a number of his officers are seen in the Chumbi Valley during the march towards the plateau.*
Photo by Royal Geographical Society

*43 bottom  This photo, dated 1905, by Bourne and Sheperd, offers a view of Everest from the highlands around Phalut in India.*
Photo: The British Library

British India, and Lord Curzon, leaving aside all other issues, committed himself to finding a solution to the Tzar's interference in Central Asia. The result was that in 1903 Colonel Francis Younghusband departed for Tibet at the head of a small army. The mission, which at the start was diplomatic, soon turned into a military intervention. The Dalai Lama abandoned Lhasa and took refuge in Mongolia. The British imposed sanctions on Tibet, and the campaign ended by blocking Russian interference. Sovereignty over the trans-Himalayan plateau—according to the two great powers—belonged to China. But it was a purely

and North Ridge of Everest, about a hundred kilometers away.

The following year, Lord Curzon revived the Everest proposal. He spoke about it to Freshfield but, curiously, continued to support an approach from Nepal. The Alpine Club showed interest, and some spoke of organising an expedition for as early as 1907, on the occasion of the fiftieth anniversary of the Club's foundation. The plan to approach Everest from Nepal was, however, soon set aside in favor of an attempt on the opposite slope, from the north. But there was a serious drawback. John Morleu, Secretary of State for India, opposed an

formal agreement, since the British did not hesitate to arm the Tibetans to keep out the soldiers of the Celestial Kingdom. Moreover, they even welcomed the Dalai Lama in India for two years, as soon as Chinese troops occupied Lhasa in 1910. This move was to have positive consequences on the concession of permits for the first British expeditions heading for Everest. During Younghusband's mission to Tibet, two facts above all had become interwoven with the question of Everest. The first was a photograph in which the East Face of Everest can be seen. It was taken by J. Claude White, an officer on the expedition, near the fortified citadel of Kamba Dzong. It was the first picture of the mountain taken from so close (only 150 kilometers). The second event concerned a small detachment of British troops at Gartok, in Western Tibet, who reported seeing the North Face

expedition to Tibet for reasons of international policy. And so the Royal Geographical Society and the Alpine Club were forced to champ at the bit. Further attempts to approach the mountain from the Nepalese side came up against the veto of the local authorities. In 1913, however, the young Captain John B. Noel, in defiance of all authorizations, carried out a clandestine sortie into Tibet, passing through Sikkim, and succeeded in observing with clarity the last 300 meters of the top cone of Everest, behind an uncharted chain of mountains. Noel was only 60 kilometers from the Himalayan giant. Until then, no Westerner had ever succeeded in drawing so close.

Only one year later, the violent winds of war swept Europe. For five years, Alpine climbing literally vanished from the minds of British subjects. This was not all: a whole generation of young

climbers in Britain was wiped out, and many of the survivors came home seriously disabled. However, right after the Armistice of 1918, the Royal Geographical Society and the Alpine Club turned their thoughts to Everest once again. The first contacts with Indian authorities were negative, but this time the plan did not fall through. In 1920 an Everest Committee was set up to organize the future expedition, to be made in Tibetan territory. Some months later, the 37-year-old Charles Kenneth Howard-Bury, a Lieutenant-Colonel in the army, set out for India. He stayed there four months, working hard in every way to obtain permission to pass through Tibet. In the end his efforts were rewarded. On 20th December 1920, Sir Francis Younghusband received a telegram: the Dalai Lama had granted permission for an expedition to Everest. The dream of the British climbers was coming true.

# THE FIRST RECONNAISSANCE
## (1921)

*44 top  Drawn up on the basis of the work carried out by Major Morshead of the Survey of India following the reconnaissance expedition of 1921, the "Preliminary Map" of Everest was included in the official book of the expedition* (Mount Everest: The Reconnaissance) *edited by C. K. Howard-Bury.* Photo: Royal Geographical Society

A few days after authorization was granted, the Royal Geographical Society and the Alpine Club were already at work. On 12th January 1921, the first meeting was called of the committee in charge of organizing the expedition which—it was said—would above all have the task of reconnaissance. Its members were well known: including Younghusband, Norman Collie, John Percy Farrar, Charles Francis Meade, plus two Honorary Secretaries: J.E.C. Eaton, for the Alpine Club, and Arthur Hinks, for the Royal Geographical Society. Two weeks later, Charles Kenneth Howard-Bury was appointed chief of the expedition and, immediately afterwards, they began to tackle the financial question, a sore point in every Himalayan journey. The British venture on Everest would cost £3-4000, and this figure was to be covered by private subscriptions within the two organizing institutions and several considerable donations. Other income was ensured by the granting of publication rights to the expedition's telegrams. The *Times* and the *Philadelphia Ledger* were to cover the event with various articles, while photographs would be ceded to the *Graphic* magazine.

The next step was to choose the climbers. Everyone wanted to take part in the expedition, but Farrar asserted himself and had his way. To start with, it was decided that topographical tasks would be entrusted to Henry T. Morshead and E. Oliver Wheeler, both of whom had good mountaineering experience. A.M. Heron, of the Geological Survey of India, would be in charge of geological studies. As far as actual climbers were concerned, however, the choice was more difficult: strong people were needed, with stamina and brilliance, but not without experience. A 56-year-old Scot, Harold Raeburn, was appointed head of the climbing team; he was an excellent Alpine climber, with previous experience in the Caucasus, and on Kangchenjunga. The other team members were Alexander Mitchell Kellas, a 53-year-old-Scot, an expert in high altitude physiology and well-acquainted with the Himalayas; A.F.R. Wollaston, 46, a doctor and well-known climber and explorer; G.H. Bullock, 34, a good climber; George Leigh Mallory, 35, who was a fairly

experienced climber, and very soon to reveal outstanding qualities as a Himalayan expert.

As far as the expedition's equipment was concerned, nothing particular was organized: these were pioneer days, and the cold and high altitude did not seem to concern the organizers over much. Each climber was left free to choose his clothing and footwear according to his personal needs. At the beginning of May the expedition was at Darjeeling, a splendid belvedere on the Himalayas, and immediately began preparations for the journey.

The plan was to cross Sikkim

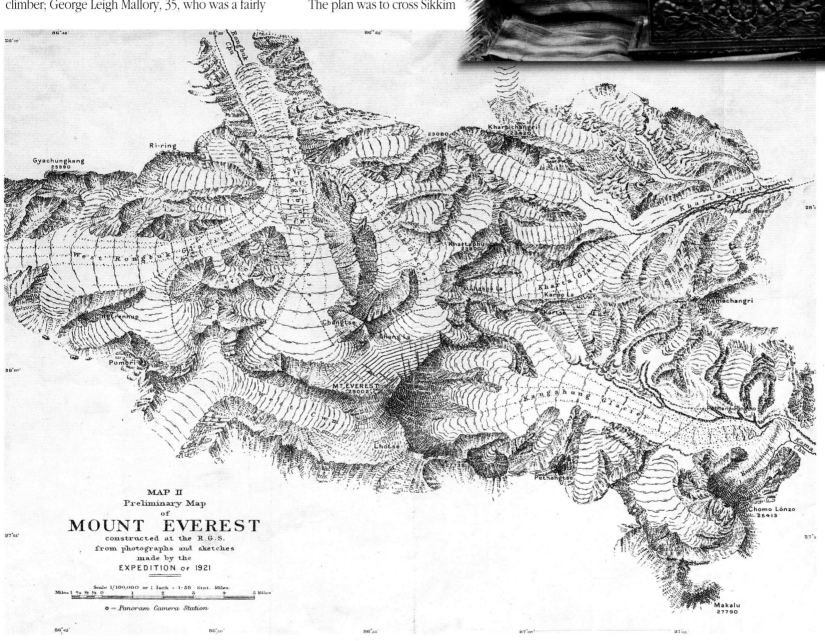

44 bottom  The climber-explorers of 1921 pose for a commemorative photo. From the left can be seen; standing, A. F. R. Wollaston, C. K. Howard-Bury, A. M. Heron, H. Raeburn; seated, G. Mallory, E. O. Wheeler, G. H. Bullock, H. T. Morshead.
Photo: Museo Nazionale della Montagna, Turin

45 center  The first detailed map of Everest was compiled on the basis of the 1921 expedition's

45 top  As well as climbing and geographical observations, the reconnaissance expedition of 1921 returned to Great Britain with fascinating documentary photos depicting life in the Tibetan highlands.
Photo: Royal Geographical Society

photographs and the notes made by the various members.
Photo: Royal Geographical Society

45 bottom  Pitched in the isolated Rongbuk Valley in sight of the glaciers and massive rock pyramid of Everest, the British expedition's base camp resembled a pioneer outpost.
Photo: Royal Geographical Society

and then, once in Tibet, to make a long march from east to west to the foot of Everest. Before setting out, on 13th May, the team of surveyors entered Sikkim with mules and porters, traveled northwards down the Tista Valley and, climbing Serpo-La, headed for Kampa Dzong in Tibet. A few days later, the second group, that of the climbers, followed a different route, which was longer but easier and more convenient for supplies. Shortly after reaching Gangtok, in an incessant downpour, Raeburn's team turned east and moved up towards the Jelep-La, a col almost 4,400 meters high,

between Sikkim and Tibet. Then the expedition went down into the Chumbi Valley, and in a few score minutes the scene changed completely. It stopped raining, the sky cleared up, and the climbers descended among forests of giant rhododendrons, amidst enchanting, luxuriant vegetation. In two days they reached Phari Dzong, at the foot of Chomolari, a gate to the Tibetan high plateaus. The caravan, now able to count on the help of donkeys, mules, horses and yaks, took the road for Kampa Dzong. It crossed Tang-La (4,630 meters), touched Dochen, crossed the Dug Pass

(5,000 meters), and reached Khe. Then came two other little cols, the higher of which was at an altitude of 5,200 meters. For some days, however, the landscape had been the semi-desert of Tibet. One last pass at about 5,270 meters, and they were at the fortified complex of Kampa Dzong where Morshead's team had been awaiting them for about a week.

The men's state of health was not the best: Wheeler and Raeburn had been complaining of serious ailments, and Kellas, a victim of dysentery, appeared very weak. His condition was worsened

*46-47 17th August 1921: the climber-explorers of the British expedition have just finished pitching a camp near Lhakpa-La, the col overlooking the eastern branch of the Rongbuk Glacier.*
Photo by Royal Geographical Society

*46 top The upper section of the Rongbuk Glacier divides into three separate branches and was an enigma for the 1921 expedition until the mystery was resolved by Mallory and Bullock in August.*
Photo: Museo Nazionale della Montagna, Turin

*46 bottom The great Rongbuk glacial flow is rather convoluted in certain stretches. The central section reaches the foot of Everest's North Face.*
Photo: Royal Geographical Society

by the fact that over the previous months he had suffered from excessive fatigue. A little rest would have helped them all, but at this point, tragedy struck. Just before reaching Kampa Dzong, Kellas died from a heart attack. A little later, it became clear that Raeburn had to return to Sikkim. His health had not improved, and Wollaston accompanied him to Lachen.

It was a moment of great distress, but Howard-Bury did not admit defeat and decided to go on. The doctors were no longer with them, it was true, but the group of surveyors was complete, and the climbing part would fall to Mallory and Bullock.

After Kampa Dzong, the expedition moved onto unknown ground, where the Survey's maps proved to be completely useless. The group moved westward, north of the Himalayan chain, opening the way into a mysterious world waiting to be explored, among sandy dunes, desert plains, some lakes and huge clouds of gnats. They reached the fort of Tinki Dzong and villages where no European had ever passed. Against the sky, to the south, day after day the great peaks of the Himalayas continued to stand out. Major Morshead and his surveyors spent all their time in making calculations and drafts to elaborate the cartography of the area. The caravan finally reached the fort of

*47 top  The topographer Oliver Wheeler, armed with a tripod and a camera, making his documentary contribution to the expedition during one of the caravan's stopovers.*
Photo: Royal Geographical Society

*47 bottom  This was how the ice-capped summit of Everest appeared to the first explorers who climbed to an altitude of just over 6,000 meters.*
Photo: Royal Geographical Society

Shekar Dzong, where, perched on the mountainside, it found a monastery with 400 monks. It was a breathtaking sight, and reminded Howard-Bury of the Mont Saint Michel headland, although the size of the Tibetan citadels was much greater.

The last stage in the long march passed through Tingri Dzong, an important trading center, which was to act as base camp. Sixty kilometers to the south the horizon appeared completely barred by the immense Himalayan chain, from which rose Everest and Cho Oyu, clearly overlooking the other peaks. Apart from the routes used by the merchants who for centuries had moved backwards and forwards between Nepal and Tibet, this apparently endless crystal garden was still to be explored. Even the access road to Chomolungma was a mystery and could be identified only with great difficulty.

The expedition soon divided into groups: Morshead remained at Tingri Dzong, to map the area, and Wollaston settled in at base camp, in the company of Howard-Bury, himself not in perfect health. Wheeler and Heron set out towards Khumbu-La to carry out topographical surveys, while Mallory and Bullock headed with determination in the direction of Everest. On 25th June the two climbers entered the valley of Rongbuk, certain of having taken the best route to approach and study the mountain.

"The Rongbuk Valley," wrote Mallory, "is well constructed to show off the peak at its head; for about 20 miles it is extraordinarily straight and in that distance rises only 4,000 feet, the glacier, which is ten miles long, no more steeply than the rest. . . . At the end of the valley and above the glacier, Everest rises not so much a peak as a prodigious mountain-mass. There is no complication for the eye. . . . To the discerning eye other mountains are visible, giants between 23,000 and 26,000 feet high. Not one of their slenderer heads even reaches their chief's shoulders. . . . "

On 26th June, the two climbers and their Sherpa porters set up a base camp just beyond the monastery of Rongbuk, at 5,000 meters, 25 kilometers south of Everest. They thought they would simply follow the glacier tongue which takes up the valley; but the chaos of crevasses and seracs forced them to seek a path on the lateral moraines. On 29th June they set up an advance camp at 5,300 meters, to explore the various branches into which the glacier divides. The solution for the ascent to the summit seemed to be the North Col, the slight depression at the base of the North Peak of Everest. But the way up was neither easy nor clear.

On 1st July Mallory explored the main valley. It was no use: perhaps the solution lay further west. Some days later, he made another attempt: five kilometers west of the camp, in an ideal position to take a look at the orography of Everest, rose Ri-Ring, a peak which reached 7,000 meters. The two men decided to climb it to plan their explorations for the following days. Once at the summit, however, they had the impression that the best way to reach the North Col was from the east, from the Kharta Valley. Unfortunately for them, they did not manage to grasp one essential detail, which is that the north ridge of Changtse breaks off after about three kilometers. As a result, the glacier which descends from the eastern slope of the North Col, changes direction of flow and heads northwest, to join the main Rongbuk branch. The mistake was to have considerable consequences on the explorations of the following weeks.

Mallory and Bullock also hypothesized a westward and southward passage, to reach the Western Cwm and attack Everest from another side. From their observation point, in fact, the Western Cwm and the Rongbuk Glacier seemed linked. And so, on 12th July, after pitching camp on the north side of the West Rongbuk Glacier, the two British climbers set off in search of the Western Cwm. Which of course they did not find. During one of their attempts at the head of the

West Rongbuk Glacier, Bullock drew near to Nup-La, the col which leads into Nepal, and some days later, continuing his wanderings at the upper end of the main glacier, he ascended to Lho-La. But at this point there could be no doubt: the geography of the area was very different from what it had appeared to the climbers from the ridge of Ri-Ring.

Having discarded the Western Cwm hypothesis, Mallory and Bullock abandoned the Rongbuk Valley to attempt an approach from the east. The rest of the expedition was waiting for them at Chobuk, and then the caravan at once took the road for Kharta, where Howard-Bury had already set up a new base camp.

The exploration started again soon afterwards. The objective, of course, was the North Col. From a different valley, another side of the gigantic mountain mass was revealed to the climbers. But once again it was not easy to find their way. A first attempt along the Kama Valley led them astray. And so the leading group turned back towards Kharta and followed the other fork, the more

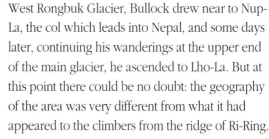

*48 top  This photograph taken during the 1921 expedition shows one of Everest's celebrated "neighbors," Cho Oyu. Located around thirty kilometers northwest of Everest, Cho Oyu (8,189 meters) was studied from 1921. Its name, of Tibetan origin, means "God of the turquoise stones."*

*48 center  Makalu (8,481), the fifth highest of the Earth's eight thousand-meter peaks, rises on the border between Tibet and Nepal, to the southeast of Everest. It was photographed during the 1921 British expedition.*

*48 bottom  A thoroughbred climber, George Mallory demonstrated a great aptitude for high altitudes in the Himalayas and notable stamina.*

northern one. Mallory, however, was feverish, and Bullock had to go on alone, although not for long.

After so much wandering about, the first doubts began to creep into the climbers' minds during those hours. Bullock was tormented by a fixed idea: the glacier which comes down eastwards from the North Col might change direction at a certain point, and heading north, might merge with the main branch at Rongbuk. Mallory did not think so. Soon afterwards, however, Howard-Bury sent one of Wheeler's topographic sketches to the camp. According to the surveyor's observations, the glacier's path coincided exactly with Bullock's suspicions. But the hypothesis of course still had to be checked. After regaining their strength, Mallory set off again together with Morshead. With a few Sherpas, the two climbers were aiming for Lakpa-La,

convinced that the solution was within reach. But up there the clouds barely enabled them to discern the descent route on the other side. But Mallory was certain this time: the road to the North Col lay that way; they just had to descend to the hollow where the glacier (which was then to be baptized with the name of East Rongbuk Glacier) started, and re-ascend the slopes on the opposite side, which however from that point were not visible. At the end of the ascent, the climbers returned to Kharta. It was the 20th August, and they had to carefully prepare the plan for the final ascent.

Ten days later, Mallory and Bullock ascended to the advance camp, waiting for the monsoon to calm. They remained stuck at 5,250 meters for three weeks, in company of the porters. But their companions soon joined them,

even Raeburn, who had just come back from Sikkim. On 21st September the weather improved. With the help of the Sherpas, Mallory and Morshead pitched a camp at Lakpa-La and this time they managed to have a look at the slopes which ascend towards the North Col.

The following day Mallory set off determinedly with Bullock and Wheeler. Morshead, Wollaston and Howard-Bury followed the leading team in case replacement was needed. Raeburn remained to look after the tents, food supplies and material at the advance camp. The groups spent the night at Lapka-La, at -34°C. At dawn, Wollaston and Howard-Bury seemed somewhat fatigued, and Morshead accompanied them to the tents further down, with several Sherpas. The others commenced the descent on the other side. They crossed the East Rongbuk Glacier and pitched another camp at 6,700 meters, below the main route up to the North Col. During the night a strong wind buffeted the tents and prevented sleep. The following morning, the little group started to climb in the direction of the Col. There were also three Sherpas, two of whom, in turn, set the pace. The first part of the way was easy; further up the slopes straightened, and progress became difficult because of the soft, deep snow. At 11.30, the team finally touched the lower platform of the North Col. Mallory wanted to climb further, but the others were too tired. The impetuous wind forced them all to descend. It was 24th September, and the icy cold of the Himalayan autumn got the better of them. The road to Everest, however, was now open.

*49 left The British climbers felt that the route to the summit would inevitably have to pass by way of the North Col.*

*49 right Seracs, icy leaps, crevasses: it was by no means easy for the 1921 expedition to identify the ascent route at the first attempt.*

*Mallory and Bullock climbed a peak that approached the 7,000-meter mark in order to gain a better view. Once in the area*

*the geography of the terrain proved to be far more complex than expected.*
Photos: Royal Geographical Society

The exploration expedition of 1921 gave a considerable boost to the Everest question. The Howard-Bury group had not yet left India when in Great Britain they were already talking of organizing a new climbing attempt for the following spring. In London the Everest Committee immediately got back to work. This time there were no great financial problems: the organization's treasury contained a large part of the funds collected for the preliminary reconnaissance, still unused.

The task of directing the new expedition was entrusted to 56-year-old General Charles Granville Bruce, a pioneer of Himalayan climbing and future President of the Alpine Club, Conway's companion in the Karakoram in 1892, Mummery's on Nanga Parbat in 1895, and who had experience in Chitral and Garhwal. Outstanding names were called upon to make up the group: Lieutenant Colonel E.L. Strutt, second only to Bruce in the expedition's hierarchy; George Mallory; George Ingle Finch, born in 1888, an excellent Alpine

mountaineer from Australia and the best climber in the team; the London surgeon Howard Somervell, age 32, a climber with inexhaustible energy; the doctor-climber Arthur William Wakefield; Edward Felix Norton, 38, with limited experience in high mountaineering, but potentially a great Himalayan climber, as he was soon to prove. The expedition's doctor was 47-year-old Tom Longstaff, who had considerable knowledge of the Himalayas. The team also included Captain John Noel, in charge of carrying out filmwork and dealing with photographic documentation; and then Geoffrey Bruce, the General's nephew, and John Morris, both officers in Gurkha divisions.

Preparations were frenzied. The departure was fixed for the end of March, so as to be able to exploit to the utmost the weeks preceding the monsoons, which usually strike Everest slightly before mid-June. Climbing equipment and clothing were chosen with care, starting with boots. Finch even made himself a rudimentary duvet filled with goosedown. Even the food supplies were different and more tasty than those of the previous year, and the menus were carefully planned to whet the climbers' appetites. Then there was the question of oxygen. Some, especially Mallory, would not hear of using it, thinking it was better to scale Everest without too much technical fuss, but others thought it was indispensable. Technicians and physiologists, who had already examined the question on behalf of the RAF, strongly urged the use of oxygen masks. Finch agreed to carry out an experiment. He performed an exercise in conditions of hypoxia, and then, in the same environment, which simulated high altitude conditions, he repeated it, using oxygen. The improvement was overwhelming, so much so that it was decided to take a certain number of oxygen cylinders on the expedition for the rope climbing on the peaks. But, from the start, there was no lack of problems, beginning with that of weight: one single apparatus—4 steel cylinders, fitted with tubes, valves, and masks—weighed 15 kilos.

The first group in the expedition left Darjeeling on 26th March; the others left a few days later. The route was the same as the previous year. The two parties rejoined at Phari Dzong, then split up again (the climbers followed a more direct route), finally meeting up at Kampa Dzong. From then on, the expedition proceeded united until Shekar Dzong,

# THE ATTEMPTS OF 1922 & 1924

*50 top  The entire 1922 expedition posing for the ritual group photo. In the center, surrounded by the climbers, is the 56-year-old General Charles*

*Granville Bruce, a pioneer of Himalayan exploration and a future president of the Alpine Club.*
Photo: Museo Nazionale della Montagna, Turin

*50 center left  By 1922 the Rongbuk Glacier was no longer the mystery it had been the previous year. However, still unexplored were the*

*central flow and the western branch heading towards Pumori.*
Photo: Museo Nazionale della Montagna, Turin

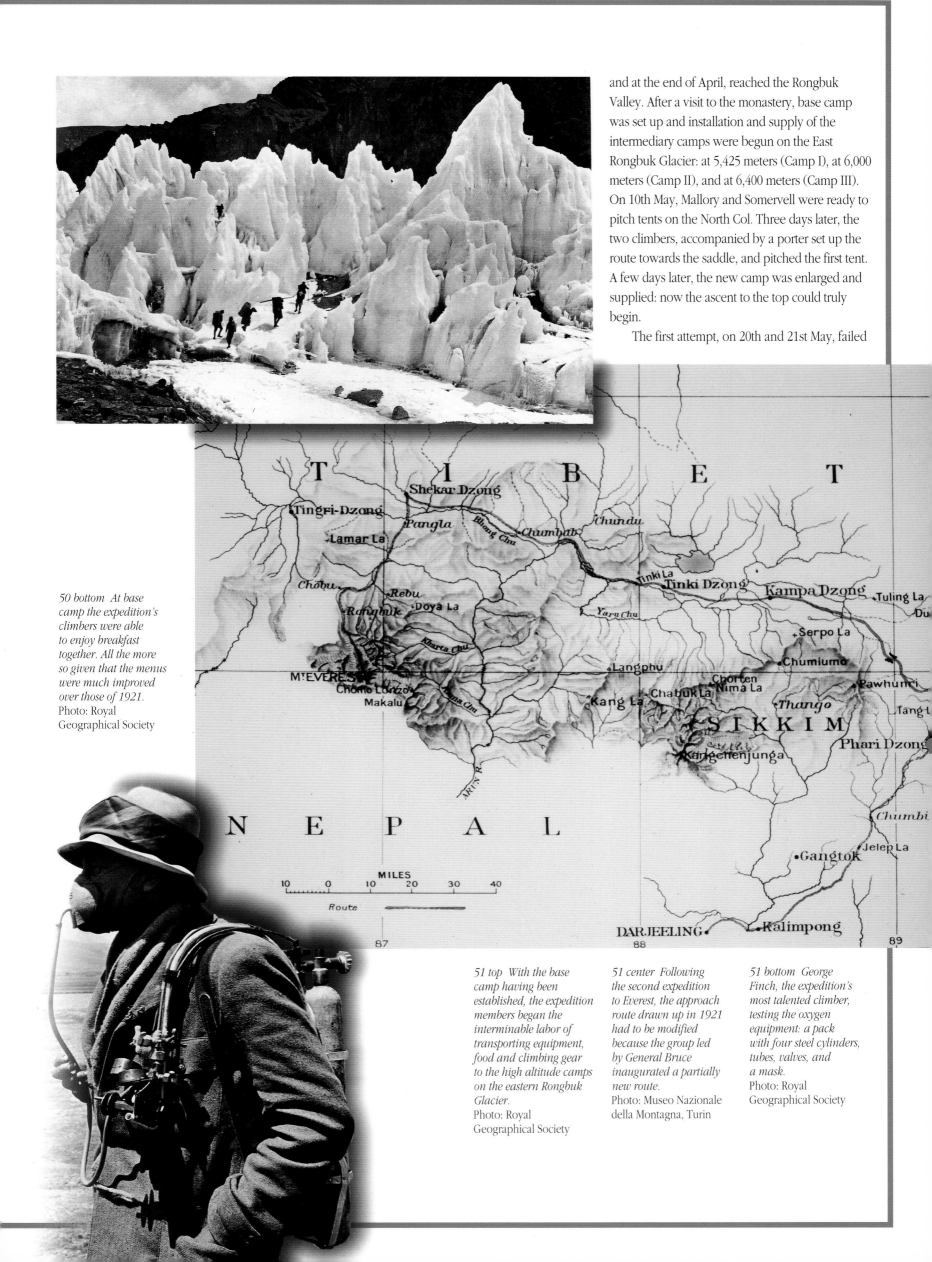

and at the end of April, reached the Rongbuk Valley. After a visit to the monastery, base camp was set up and installation and supply of the intermediary camps were begun on the East Rongbuk Glacier: at 5,425 meters (Camp I), at 6,000 meters (Camp II), and at 6,400 meters (Camp III). On 10th May, Mallory and Somervell were ready to pitch tents on the North Col. Three days later, the two climbers, accompanied by a porter set up the route towards the saddle, and pitched the first tent. A few days later, the new camp was enlarged and supplied: now the ascent to the top could truly begin.

The first attempt, on 20th and 21st May, failed

*50 bottom At base camp the expedition's climbers were able to enjoy breakfast together. All the more so given that the menus were much improved over those of 1921.*
Photo: Royal Geographical Society

*51 top With the base camp having been established, the expedition members began the interminable labor of transporting equipment, food and climbing gear to the high altitude camps on the eastern Rongbuk Glacier.*
Photo: Royal Geographical Society

*51 center Following the second expedition to Everest, the approach route drawn up in 1921 had to be modified because the group led by General Bruce inaugurated a partially new route.*
Photo: Museo Nazionale della Montagna, Turin

*51 bottom George Finch, the expedition's most talented climber, testing the oxygen equipment: a pack with four steel cylinders, tubes, valves, and a mask.*
Photo: Royal Geographical Society

due to their inexperience. Mallory thought that, to reach the summit, only one camp, one thousand meters higher up, would be sufficient. But the high altitude and lack of oxygen slowed down progress, and the leading team—Mallory, Somervell, Norton and Morshead—spent the night lower down than planned, at 7,600 meters. The following day, Morshead gave up, the others continued to 8,170 meters, and then again took the way down to the North Col. At first sight, the descent seemed easy, but a mistake in bearings, Morshead's poor health, and a dangerous slip turned it into a nightmare. The group regained Camp IV in the middle of the night, at 23.30. The climbers were dropping with fatigue, hunger and thirst. They were all dehydrated, but there were no pans in which to cook or make tea: by mistake the Sherpas had taken them all back down. Norton mixed condensed milk with jam and snow: definitely a terrible concoction for the stomach, but nonetheless better than starving at high altitude. The following morning, after a difficult night struggling against the pangs of hunger and thirst, the party reached Camp III, laying tracks in the

fresh snow. At the tents, where they drank litres of boiling tea, the climbers met Finch, Geoffrey Bruce and the Gurkha Tejbir, who were ready to set out for the North Col, with oxygen cylinders and equipment.

This was only a first experiment, but in point of fact, Finch and Bruce succeeded in showing their companions—almost all skeptical—that the oxygen masks were invaluable. With the help of the "English air," they reached the Col in three hours and came back to camp in less than 50 minutes. A great performance, and also a good investment for their attempt on the summit.

Two days later, on 24th May, Finch, Bruce, Tejbir and Noel started out again for the North Col, with the intention of climbing to the summit of Everest. Noel stopped at Camp IV, but his companions continued with determination upwards. At the same time, a group of porters, laden with oxygen cylinders, climbed up to 7,800 meters. At that point, on the ridge, the climbers pitched a tent and spent the night buffeted by the increasing wind. The following morning, the windstorm had still not ceased. They should have descended, but

*52 top left This photo was distributed throughout the world: George Mallory and Edward Felix Norton where photographed by Somervell at an altitude of just under 8,200 meters on the North side of Everest. All three were climbing without oxygen.*
Photo: Royal Geographical Society

*52 bottom left One of the two attempts on the summit of 1922, that of Finch and Bruce along the Gurkha Tejbir, was made with the aid of oxygen. Technical experts and physiologists had strongly advised the climbers to use breathing gear.*
Photo: Royal Geographical Society

*52 right The camp pitched on the North Col, an obligatory passage on the way to the ridge, represented a shelter of fundamental importance for the expedition's climbers (the northeast shoulder of Everest can be seen at the top).*
Photo: Royal Geographical Society

*53 top left A roped party composed of numerous climbers and Sherpas burdened with heavy packs descending as best they can along the icy slope near the Chang-La Saddle, the North Col.*
Photo: Royal Geographical Society

*53 top right  In contrast with what the first explorers of Everest had thought, the Western Cwm, the high glacial basin opening onto the Nepalese side of the mountain, is not connected to the Rongbuk Glacier.*
Photo: Royal Geographical Society

*53 bottom  Geoffrey Bruce (the nephew of the expedition leader), having pushed on to an extremely high altitude during a resolute attempt on the summit, is being helped by the Sherpas during his descent.*
Photo: Salkeld Collection

the group did not want to give up and decided to wait. In the late afternoon, sent up by Noel, six Sherpas climbed to the little camp on the ridge, bringing hot tea and soup.

The second night was terribly cold. Finch used the oxygen to ensure the group's survival, sorely tried by their stay at high altitude. The idea worked; so well that the following morning, the climbers got up early and set out towards the summit. Tejbir, more laden than the others, had the task of climbing to the point where the North Ridge joins the Northeast one, but he gave up at 7,900 meters and returned to the tent. Bruce and Finch continued unroped. When the wind started blowing again, the two climbers abandoned the ridge to continue on the north side, which was more sheltered. On the rocky slabs of the Yellow Band, Bruce, less experienced than his companion, moved too slowly. At 8,200 meters, Finch decided to return to the ridge. Shortly afterwards, however, Bruce halted: his oxygen equipment was no longer working and the damage had to be repaired immediately. But time was passing and at 8,320 meters the climbers soon decided to retreat. Roped together, they quickly returned to Camp V. Tejbir remained to wait for the Sherpas who were coming up to take down the tent; his companions continued the descent to the North Col, where they refreshed themselves before starting out for Camp III. The expedition had a tragic epilogue: on 7th June during a new attempt after the early arrival of the monsoon, four rope parties—Mallory, Somervell, Crawford and thirteen Sherpas—were struck by an avalanche below the North Col. Seven porters were killed. From base camp, General Bruce ordered retreat.

The second climbing attempt on Everest took place in 1924. Two years after the previous expedition, time now seemed ripe for the final ascent. The experience accumulated during the spring of 1922, the first experiments with oxygen and the altitude reached gave much room for hope. It was clear that the whole climb must proceed with careful, accurate progress starting from the North Col. A precise plan with strategy studied right down to the last detail had to be made.

The new expedition was again directed by General Bruce. Edward Norton was appointed second-in-charge. The others chosen were Mallory, of course, now an Everest veteran, Somervell, John Noel, Geoffrey Bruce, the geologist Noel Odell, the doctor-climber Bentley Beetham, John de Vere Hazard, the very young Andrew Irvine, and lastly E.O. Shebbeare and Dr. R.W.G. Hingston, respectively responsible for transport supervision and the climbers' health.

The group set out from Darjeeling on 25th March. The route was the usual one, and everything seemed to be going smoothly.

Only two weeks later, however, Bruce went down with malarial fever and was forced to return to base. The command of the expedition was taken over by Norton who, together with Mallory, decided on the ascent plan. The idea was to equip three camps after the North Col, Camps V, VI and VII, at respectively 7,750, 8,000 and 8,300 meters; and to make two simultaneous attempts at the final ascent. One group would start from Camp VI (with oxygen), and the other from Camp VII (without cylinders); the two teams would help each other out. Norton also decided the summit rope parties: Mallory and Irvine, with oxygen cylinders and masks; Somervell and Norton, without oxygen. For Mallory, apart from personal feelings of friendship, the choice of Irvine was almost compulsory, because he was one of the few members of the team who knew everything about the functioning and maintenance of the oxygen equipment.

On 28th April, the expedition reached Rongbuk. Norton calculated that the first attempt on the summit would be made

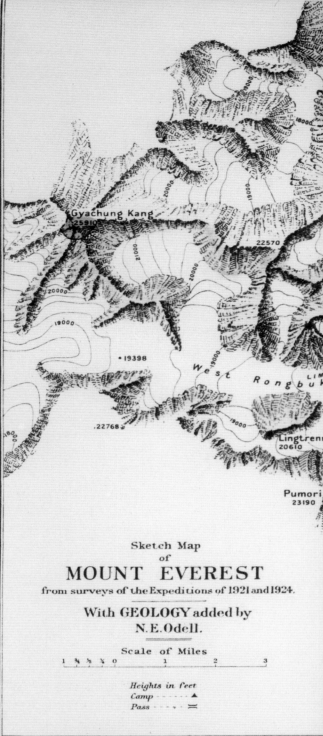

54  This photo portrays some of the members of the 1924 Everest expedition, from the left (standing): A. Irvine, G. L. Mallory, E. F. Norton, N. E. Odell, J. MacDonald; (seated) E. O. Shebbeare, G. C. Bruce, T. H. Somervell, B. Beetham. Figures of great significance such as G. Bruce, J. de Vere Hazard and R. W. G. Hingston are missing, however.
Photo: Royal Geographical Society

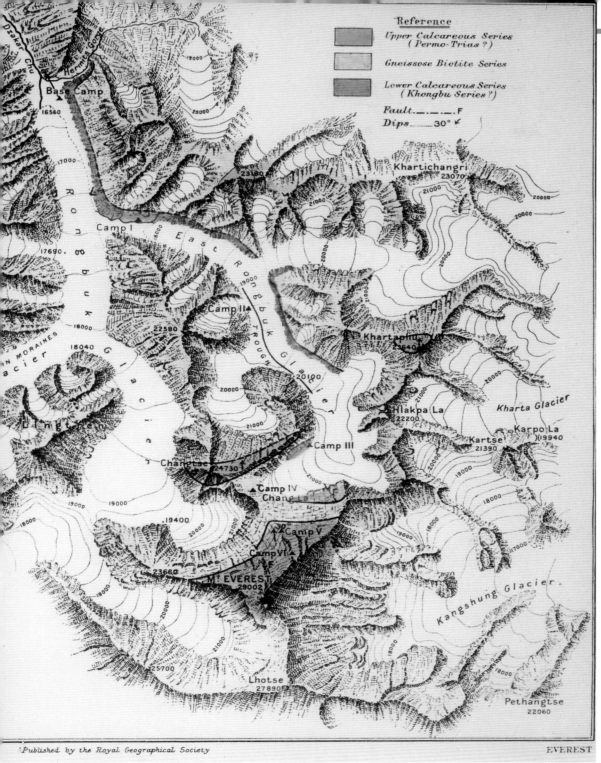

Reference

Upper Calcareous Series
( Permo-Trias ? )

Gneissose Biotite Series

Lower Calcareous Series
( Khongbu Series ? )

Fault._____F

Dips_____30°

*Published by the Royal Geographical Society*

EVEREST

54-55 *The various
expeditions led to
increasingly detailed
knowledge of the
geography of the region
surrounding Everest and
ever more accurate maps.*
Photo: Royal
Geographical Society

55 top *Ascending the
Rongbuk Valley, the
silhouette of Everest
standing out against the
horizon becomes ever
larger and breathtakingly
powerful.*
Photo: Museo Nazionale
della Montagna, Turin

55 bottom *With the
geographical problems
having been solved,
the camps in the eastern
branch of the Rongbuk
Glacier became routine
stops for the climbers
of the prewar British
expeditions.*
Photo: Royal
Geographical Society

around 17th May: the likelihood of the
monsoon arriving early, as it had in 1922,
advised them to speed things up. The first
camps were set up with the help of 150 local
porters, to spare the Sherpas and climbers. The
schedule seemed perfect, but the bad weather
put its spoke in and, between the second and
third camps, the expedition encountered
serious difficulties. Temperatures fell to Arctic
levels, the wind ceaselessly swept the glaciers,
and the transport operations came to a
complete halt. Norton ordered a general
descent to base camp, to wait for
meteorological conditions to improve.
Hingston and Somervell treated the Gurkhas
and Sherpas for various ailments and frostbite,
but could not save two men from death.

On 15th May, the lama of the Rongbuk
monastery met the expedition and blessed both
climbers and bearers. Shortly afterwards the
weather began to improve and new plans for
the ascent were made. Four days later, the first
three camps were again occupied.

Immediately, Mallory and Norton, followed by Odell and the Sherpa Lhakpa attacked the slopes of the North Col. They mapped out a route which was different from the one used two years previously, and set it with several fixed ropes. The following morning, Somervell, Irvine and Hazard climbed the Col in their turn with a group of Sherpas and set up Camp IV. But the next day it again began to snow heavily, and the group abandoned the tents. They all descended, except for four Sherpas, who were frightened by the steepness of the slopes.

The monsoon seemed to have arrived. Worried about the fate of the Sherpas stuck at Camp IV, Norton worked out a rescue operation. Norton, Mallory and Somervell, the most experienced, acclimatized climbers in the expedition, succeeded in bringing the four men down. The next day the weather gave no hint of

improving. The mountain was truly unclimbable, and Camp III was also evacuated. After yet another retreat, the expedition seemed to be on the point of failing. But suddenly the sky cleared and the fine weather returned: it was clear that the snowstorms had nothing to do with the monsoon.

There was only one thing they could do: make an all out attempt, laying aside all previous plans. Even the oxygen was forgotten: to lighten the transport loads, they had to do without it. Mallory and Geoffrey Bruce decided to make a first attempt. Behind them would follow Somervell and Norton, while Odell and Irvine, lower down, would look after the tents at the North Col, with Noel's help.

On 30th May, the leading rope parties of the expedition were all at Camp III. The following day Mallory and Bruce reset the way to the North Col and settled in at Camp IV. On 1st June, they attacked the ridge, followed by the Sherpas. At 7,600 meters, half of the porters laid down their packs and descended. Camp V was set up a hundred meters or so higher up. Mallory, Bruce and four Sherpas settled into the two tents.

On the following day, Norton, Somervell and a few Sherpas succeeded in their turn in climbing the ridge. The wind was merciless, and they soon met Mallory's group coming down towards the North Col. At 13.00 hours, Norton and his men reached Camp V. The next day, surprisingly, the storm decreased in intensity and the group was able to start to ascend again. At 8,170 meters, they pitched a new camp, the sixth.

On the following morning, the weather was perfect and there was no wind. Norton and Somervell felt fit and at 6.40 started out for the summit. Only one hour later they reached the Yellow Band, and soon began to feel the altitude: their progress slowed down, Somervell had difficulty in breathing due to a sore throat, and Norton had eyesight problems because he had forgotten to use dark glasses. The two climbers however succeeded in passing the limestone

rocks of the Yellow Band. They crossed the North Face of Everest, keeping 150-200 meters below the Northeast Ridge, and at midday drew near to the great gully situated at the base of the summit cone. Somervell halted, while Norton continued to 8,573 meters, a record in altitude. But the summit was still too far off. They were forced to descend.

Norton took an hour to get back to the place where Somervell was waiting for him. The ground was treacherous; in fact, to reach his companion, he had to throw one end of the rope to him. Shortly afterwards, roped together, the two climbers began their descent. They proceeded fairly quickly to Camp VI, took down the tent and continued down. At Camp V, they decided to continue to the North Col. On the last stage of the ridge, by then over their difficulty, the climbers unroped. Norton descended with no difficulty, but behind him Somervell seemed to be suffocating:

*56 top  For the Everest veterans, the pitching of the base camp within sight of the Himalayan giant was by now a kind of ritual, as was the visit to the lama at the Rongbuk monastery.*

*56 bottom  The young Andrew Irvine was appointed as the expedition's oxygen equipment technician, a task he performed perfectly.*

*56-57 Where possible the high altitude camps were pitched out of the wind and sheltered from the driving snow that sweeps the glaciers and the north side of Everest. The climbers tried to take advantage of piles of rock, seracs and ridge lines.*

*57 top left  Following the establishment of Camp III, the 1924 British expedition suffered a set-back: a long period of bad weather obliged all the climbers to retreat back down the valley for a number of days.*

*57 top  From one expedition to the next the Sherpas employed by the various groups improved their climbing technique and learned how to use ropes, ice axes and crampons.*

Photos: Royal Geographical Society

he could no longer breathe and coughed continuously. He thought he was dying. Finally, in desperation, he gave himself a hard blow on the chest and suddenly felt a plug of mucus rise in his throat. The effort made his throat bleed, but he could breathe again. Shortly afterwards, in the light of an electric torch, Norton and Somervell continued their way down. At their shouts, Mallory and Odell arrived and accompanied them to the camp, where Irvine was busy cooking. During the night, Norton was seized with blinding pain in his eyes: this was the first symptom of the ophthalmia which was to make him completely blind for sixty hours.

On the following days, the weather

camp. Just below, Odell and the Sherpas in turn reached Camp V, where they met, on their way down, the Sherpas who had followed Mallory and Irvine. Everything went well: the head rope was in good shape, the weather was fine and all the higher camps were occupied by the climbers.

On 8th June, Mallory and Irvine finally set off for the summit. It is hard to say at what time they left the tents: we may only guess. Meanwhile, further down, Odell set off towards Camp VI. The sky was clear, but at about 8.00 hours some clouds coming from the west prevented them from seeing in detail the upper part of the ridge which stretches to the summit of Everest. At 7,900 meters, Odell climbed to the top of a

*58 left  In order to climb to the North Col, the 1924 expedition used the Chimney Route, a rather difficult itinerary that slips through a gap between high seracs; in recompense the route is protected from avalanches.*
Photo: Royal Geographical Society

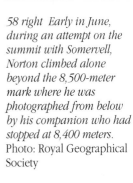

*58 right  Early in June, during an attempt on the summit with Somervell, Norton climbed alone beyond the 8,500-meter mark where he was photographed from below by his companion who had stopped at 8,400 meters.*
Photo: Royal Geographical Society

*58-59  This shot of the North Face of Everest allows us to identify the highest point reached by the British climbers during the two attempts on the summit made in June 1924.*
Photo: Royal Geographical Society

continued to stay fine, and the Sherpas again took up the work of supplying the higher camps. There might be one more chance of success. In the end, Mallory decided to try again, this time with the oxygen equipment. They would do without up to Camp VI, and then use the cylinders. Norton advised him to climb with Odell, by now well-acclimatized, but Mallory did not agree. He preferred to rope with Irvine. And so it was. On 6th June, the two climbers set off towards Camp V, together with eight Sherpas. The following day, they ascended to the sixth

pinnacle. It was 12.50 hours and suddenly, very clearly, the upper part of the Himalayan giant appeared. Far away, on a snowy slope which leads towards a projection of the ridge, before the final pyramid, he spotted a dark dot moving, then a second: Mallory and Irvine, without a doubt. But it was not easy to fix accurately the point where the climbers were, and in fact the clouds quickly closed over. Subsequently, with the help of some photographs of the face, the altitude was estimated at around 8,450 meters.

At 14.00 hours, when Odell reached Camp

VI, the wind rose and it began to snow. Soon visibility became a problem. Thinking Mallory and Irvine were probably on their way back, the climber ascended for about fifty meters above the camp and shouted several times. No reply. He stayed for a long time waiting for his companions, and then went back to the tent. Two hours after its beginning, the blizzard calmed down and the sun came out again. Odell observed the ridge and wall for a long time without seeing the least trace of the two climbing to the summit.

Camp VI 26,700
about here

Norton & Somervell
about here 28,130
June 4.

Mallory & Irvine
last seen about here 28,230
June 8.

Then he descended, to leave the tent free for the rope party of the late-comers. Moreover, according to Mallory's instructions, he was also supposed to leave Camp V free, and so was forced to descend to the North Col, where Hazard was waiting for him. For the whole night the two men stared at the ridge, with the hope of pinpointing their companions' location. There was no sign, not even the next morning. And so at midday, Odell and two Sherpas started out for the two higher camps. They spent the night at Camp V, then, the following day, with the help of oxygen, Odell continued alone up to the highest tent. But not even at Camp VI was there the slightest sign of Mallory and Irvine.

What had happened? It was pointless, at that moment, to make any guesses; it was better to go on up. Odell continued upwards with the strength of desperation, in the hope of finding some trace. Still nothing. Two hours later he gave up. He placed two sleeping bags on the snow in a T shape, so that Hazard, from Camp IV, would know the outcome of his search. In the meantime Norton, Bruce, Noel and Hingston waited for news at Camp III. Back at the North Col, Odell prepared another signal for the expedition chief, lining up six blankets in the shape of a cross. Norton replied to give up the search. The expedition was over, it was useless to risk other lives. No one will ever know whether Mallory and Irvine succeeded in reaching the summit of Everest.

Dear Noel,
We'll probably start early to-morrow (8th) in order to have clear weather. It won't be too early to start looking out for us either crossing the rock band under the pyramid or going up skyline at 8.0 p.m.
Yr ever
G Mallory

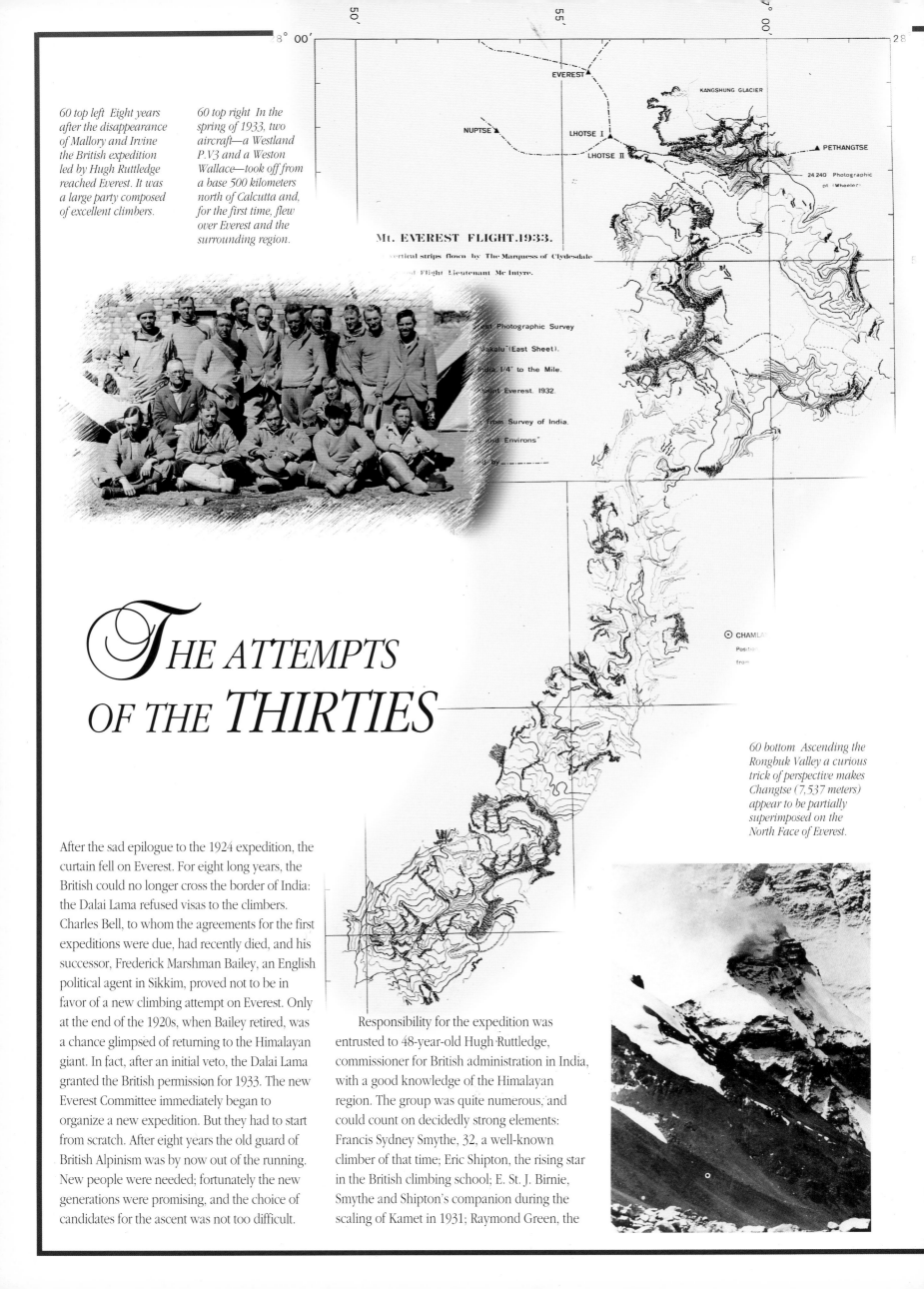

*60 top left Eight years after the disappearance of Mallory and Irvine the British expedition led by Hugh Ruttledge reached Everest. It was a large party composed of excellent climbers.*

*60 top right In the spring of 1933, two aircraft—a Westland P.V3 and a Weston Wallace—took off from a base 500 kilometers north of Calcutta and, for the first time, flew over Everest and the surrounding region.*

EVEREST

KANGSHUNG GLACIER

NUPTSE

LHOTSE I

LHOTSE II

PETHANGTSE

24 240 Photographic pt (Wheeler)

Mt. EVEREST FLIGHT.1933.

vertical strips flown by The Marquess of Clydesdale
and Flight Lieutenant Mc Intyre.

est Photographic Survey
akalu"(East Sheet).
India, 1/4" to the Mile.
unt Everest. 1932.

from Survey of India.
nd Environs"

by

CHAMLA

Position

from

# *T*HE ATTEMPTS OF THE *THIRTIES*

*60 bottom Ascending the Rongbuk Valley a curious trick of perspective makes Changtse (7,537 meters) appear to be partially superimposed on the North Face of Everest.*

After the sad epilogue to the 1924 expedition, the curtain fell on Everest. For eight long years, the British could no longer cross the border of India: the Dalai Lama refused visas to the climbers. Charles Bell, to whom the agreements for the first expeditions were due, had recently died, and his successor, Frederick Marshman Bailey, an English political agent in Sikkim, proved not to be in favor of a new climbing attempt on Everest. Only at the end of the 1920s, when Bailey retired, was a chance glimpsed of returning to the Himalayan giant. In fact, after an initial veto, the Dalai Lama granted the British permission for 1933. The new Everest Committee immediately began to organize a new expedition. But they had to start from scratch. After eight years the old guard of British Alpinism was by now out of the running. New people were needed; fortunately the new generations were promising, and the choice of candidates for the ascent was not too difficult.

Responsibility for the expedition was entrusted to 48-year-old Hugh Ruttledge, commissioner for British administration in India, with a good knowledge of the Himalayan region. The group was quite numerous, and could count on decidedly strong elements: Francis Sydney Smythe, 32, a well-known climber of that time; Eric Shipton, the rising star in the British climbing school; E. St. J. Birnie, Smythe and Shipton's companion during the scaling of Kamet in 1931; Raymond Green, the doctor responsible for the whole team; Dr. W. MacLean; Colin Crawford, a veteran of the 1922 expedition; Percy Wyn-Harris, a good Alpine climber, though without experience in the Himalayas; Laurence Wager and Jack Longland, two pedigreed climbers; Major Hugh Boustead, an adventurer who knew Sikkim well; T.A. Brockleband, 24, Alpine climber and canoeing champion; George Wood-Johnson, who had been part of the international expedition to Kangchenjunga in 1931; E.O. Shebbeare, a liaison officer with great experience, a survivor of the 1924 attempt; and two telegraph officers (wireless communications were a novelty in Himalayan climbing), E.C. Thompson and W.R. Smith-Windham.

The equipment was chosen with a certain care for the occasion, especially as far as the tents and windproof clothing (the latter was also supplied for the high altitude porters) were concerned. Eight years after the last Everest expedition, equipment had not been greatly improved, although some progress had been made. Any innovations in 1933 lay elsewhere: first and foremost a better knowledge of high altitude Himalayan climbing (previous experience, including mistakes made, turned out to be invaluable), and then the technical improvement of the Sherpas, now used by the foremost world climbers on the highest Himalayan peaks. As far as oxygen was concerned, the new equipment had become much lighter (although the expedition of 1933 never used it during the ascent).

The approach march of the Ruttledge expedition was uneventful, except for the dates, which were decidedly earlier than usual: departure

from Darjeeling at the end of February, arrival at Rongbuk on 16th April. To avoid exhausting their strength struggling against bad weather conditions, the first camps were pitched quite slowly. The ascent to the North Col demanded great effort and a great deal of time, because the glacier slopes had considerably altered—for the worse. The technical problem of access to the saddle—a vertical wall which was also a sheer drop—was brilliantly solved by Smythe, the best glacier climber in the group. On 13th May the

*61 left Hugh Boustead and George Wood-Johnson roped together as they ascend the upper section of the eastern branch of the Rongbuk Glacier. Both men were well versed in Himalayan climbing. Wood-Johnson in particular, as in 1931 he had taken part in the international expedition to Kangchenjunga.*

*61 right By 1933 the slopes that gave access to the North Col had become steeper and the ascent route had to be equipped with a ladder to aid the passage of the heavily loaded porters.*

Photos: Royal Geographical Society

*62 left  An ascent of Everest is above all a grueling enterprise with much coming and going on the mountain, transporting materials, tents and foodstuffs prior to the final assault on the summit.*

*62 right  At the first sign of numbness due to the low temperatures at high altitudes the circulation in the limbs must be restored to prevent frostbite.*

*63 top left  Captain E. St. J. Birnie, immobilized in his tent at Camp II by frostbite affecting his lower limbs, is carried by the Sherpas towards the Everest base camp.*

*63 bottom left  A party of climbers and porters struggling to clear a path through fresh snow following a prolonged period of bad weather, a thankless task that drains the energy of even the fittest climbers.*

*63 right  From Camp V above the North Col, at 7,700 meters, the panorama is spectacularly broad in good weather. The notable altitude means that both sides of the ridge can be seen together with the most distant mountains.*

Photos: Royal Geographical Society

Birnie), helped by a small group of Sherpas, pitched a new camp, the sixth, at 8,350 meters. In the afternoon, Longland descended with the porters. But it was hell: a terrible blizzard was sweeping the mountain, the way was difficult to find, visibility was almost nil. In the end, when it seemed there was nothing they could do, Longland's experience and skill won out, and the group succeeded in gaining the tents of Camp V.

After a sleepless night, at 5.40 the following morning, Wager and Wyn-Harris started out for the summit. They climbed diagonally towards the Northeast Ridge. One hour later, they came across an ice-axe leaning against an outcrop of rock: without a doubt (the manufacturer's name was stamped on the handle), it was Mallory's or Irvine's. It was the only trace of the tragedy of 1924. Immediately afterwards, the two climbers

Wager, on reaching the ridge beneath the First Step, had a look at the gigantic East Face, Wyn-Harris retrieved the ice-axe found on their way up. At 16.00 the climbers were once more at Camp VI, where they met Smythe and Shipton, and then continued down to the tents of Camp V. In the meantime the weather had changed again. Smythe and Shipton only managed to set out for the summit on the morning of 1st June. But they were not in good shape: the two nights spent at high altitudes had tired them both, especially Shipton, who halted at the base of the First Step and turned back. Smythe however continued alone, along the route opened up by Norton. The ground was not difficult, but turned out to be treacherous. Having reached the same altitude as Wager and Wyn-Harris, he decided to descend. If he had used oxygen, perhaps . . . His failure, however, was not

passage was secured with a fixed rope; and the following day, despite the wind, a team of climbers and porters set up Camp IV. A blizzard started shortly afterwards, and lasted without a break for several days, keeping the men in their tents. In the meantime, the news reached them by telegraph that the monsoons were raging in the Bay of Bengal. There was just time for one attempt on the summit, as long as the wind did not blow too violently.

On 22nd May Camp V was set up, at 7,830 meters. Wyn-Harris, Greene, Boustead and Wager remained there. The following day Smythe and Shipton climbed up, taking the places of Wager and Wyn-Harris. But it was hopeless: the wind blew strongly for two days, and the entire group descended to the North Col.

The ascent started again on 28th May, when Birnie, Longland, Wager and Wyn-Harris settled into Camp V. On the 29th, three of them (without

aimed for the First Step of the ridge. They soon realized, however, that moving along the edge of the ridge was too difficult. So they continued lower down, along the Yellow Band, with the intention of climbing straight up over the Second Step. The latter appeared before them as a formidable vertical wall. And so they crossed downwards, on difficult ground, towards the Norton Couloir. The gully was full of powdery snow, but fortunately they managed to cross it. Once past the couloir, 15 meters above the Yellow Band, they stopped: it was 12.30 and the summit of Everest was 300 meters above them. The altitude was roughly that reached by Norton in 1924 and, in good conditions, it would take them four hours of climbing to reach the summit. But the rocks were covered with hard snow, and to progress further seemed dangerous. Wager and Wyn-Harris gave up. They went down by a different, easier path from that of the ascent. While

only due to exhaustion: we must also take into account the psychological stress and lack of that mental clarity necessary to climb. In the last part of the climb, in fact, Smythe experienced a sort of hallucination and had the feeling he was walking alongside a companion who was following him step by step. Furthermore, during the descent to Camp VI, he repeatedly saw two dark objects hanging in the air, which seemed to slowly palpitate. Having reached the tent, Smythe felt too tired to go on. Shipton, however, took the path for Camp V. But it was amazing that he managed to reach his destination, because a violent blizzard made him lose his bearings completely.

The following day, which was not without problems (another blizzard), Smythe arrived at the fifth camp, just abandoned by Shipton and Birnie, and then continued down to the North Col. On 7th June, the entire expedition met up at the base camp: the prelude to their return to Darjeeling.

The following year a singular event was recorded: Maurice Wilson, an eccentric former officer in the British Army, moved by mystical motives, attempted to climb Everest alone. His body was found the following spring at 6,400 meters, near a food depot abandoned by the 1933 expedition.

In 1935 the British organized a new expedition, aimed at broadening geographic knowledge of the mountain and at making an in-depth study of the best route for the final ascent.

Directed by Shipton, the group included Harold William Tilman, a fine explorer-climber (the previous year he had explored the Nanda Devi basin with Shipton), Dr. Charles Warren, Edwin Kempson, Edmund Wigram, the topographer Michael Spencer and New Zealander L.V. Bryant, all excellent climbers.

*65 bottom left  During the exploration of the Everest region in 1935, Eric Shipton and Dan Bryant pushed on towards the Lingtren Group where they climbed three new peaks (the mountain in the photo is the 6,437-meter summit). Photo: Royal Geographical Society*

*65 bottom right  In just two months the Shipton expedition scaled no less than 26 peaks, explored the three branches of the Rongbuk Glacier and visited other areas in the region as well as contributing to the cartographic surveys. Photo: Royal Geographical Society*

The group of Sherpas was joined at the last moment by 20-year-old Tenzing Norgay, a young man who seemed to be promising material.

The caravan set off from Darjeeling at the end of May and, from the start, carried out explorations into unknown territory, avoiding the usual approach route. That year the monsoons arrived late—on 26th June—and good weather conditions remained on Everest for a long time. But Shipton remained faithful to his schedule and did not allow himself to be tempted by the summit. This was not surprising, because his interests had turned towards exploration, away from the ascent of the Himalayan giant, and he seized every opportunity that year to explore unknown corners of the Himalayan region.

As far as Everest was concerned, the expedition moved with incredible speed: it thoroughly studied the slopes giving access to the North Col and, in only six days from Rongbuk, set up Camp IV. Then the group turned elsewhere. In two months it ascended 26 peaks and crossed the three branches of the Rongbuk Glacier lengthways and crosswise. At the beginning of August Tilman and Wigram climbed to Lho-La and studied the West Ridge of Everest, while Shipton and Bryant reclimbed the West Glacier and scaled three peaks of the Lingtren Group, from where they could easily observe the Western Cwm. Spender and Warren, instead, carried out cartographic sketches of the region, furthering the work already started in the 1920s. In 1936 there was another expedition to Everest. The team leader was again Ruttledge, who called on eight climbers with well-proven experience: Smythe, Shipton, Wyn-Harris, Kempson, Warren, Wigram, joined by P.R. Oliver and J.M.L. Gravin, both excellent climbers. John Morris, the liaison officer already following the 1922 expedition, was also part of the group, as were radio operator W.R. Smyth-Windham and Dr. G. Noel Humphreys.

*66-67 While exploring westwards Shipton and his companions photographed a new view of Everest that also included Nuptse.*
Photo: Royal Geographical Society

*66 bottom left During the 1935 expedition Eric Shipton and Dan Bryant climbed three peaks in the Lingtren Group from where they were easily able to observe the glacial expanse of the Western Cwm on the Nepalese side of Everest.*
Photo: Alpine Club Library Collection

*67 top Eric Shipton, the leader of the 1935 expedition and an untiring Himalayan explorer, photographed by his climbing partner at an altitude of 6,400 meters on the glacier.*
Photo: Royal Geographical Society

*66 bottom right After having forgone ascents beyond the North Col on Shipton's orders, the climbers on the 1935 expedition carefully explored the area surrounding Everest. They also completed a number of climbs in the area around Camp II (in the photo) on the East Rongbuk Glacier.*
Photo: Royal Geographical Society

*67 center During the various exploratory climbs made by the Shipton expedition Everest was photographed from different viewpoints, as in the case of this shot taken at an altitude of 6,931 meters to the north of the East Rongbuk Glacier.*
Photo: Royal Geographical Society

*67 bottom Having cleared the Kartha Phu Col, the Shipton expedition explored the Kartha and Karthchangri Glaciers, adding significant detail to the cartography of the area.*
Photo: Royal Geographical Society

THE NORTHERN FACE OF MOUNT EVEREST
based on Photogrammetric Surveys by Michaël Spender

Scale 1/20000

Yards
200   0   200   400   600   800   1000   1200

Metres
200   0   200   400   600   800   1000   1200

Heights in feet and approximate contours
by stereo-photogrammetry.

Summit
29002
28840   28700   28000   27000
28180
Foot of Second Step   26000
28140   27650
Foot of First Step   26000
27950   25000

North East Shoulder
27510

27000
26000
25000
24000
24000
23000
23000
22000
22000
21000
21000

Chang La
22990
North Col

R o n

East Rongbuk Glacier

21760   North Peak
24740

*68-69 On the basis of the stereogrammetrical surveys completed by the topographer Michael Spencer, a member of the Shipton expedition, a detailed map of the northern side of Everest was drawn up, the most precise to have been published at that time.*

*68 bottom left The group of Sherpas that accompanied the expedition was composed of men of great experience including Ang Tarkay and Ang Thering. Among the younger members was Tenzing Bothia, subsequently known as Tenzing Norgay, Hillary's companion in 1953.*

*68 bottom right The British expedition of 1936 led by Hugh Ruttledge was composed of excellent climbers. In this photo taken at base camp the following figures can be recognized: (standing, left to right) W. R. Smyth-Windham, P. R. Oliver, G. N. Humphreys, C. B. M. Warren; (center) E. Shipton, F. S. Smythe, H. Ruttledge, C. J. Morris, P. Wyn-Harris; (seated) J. Gravin, E. H. L. Wigram, E. G. H. Kempson.*

*69 top Camp III at the bottom of the slopes giving access to the western side of Chang-La, was established by the Ruttledge expedition early in May. From here on the 13th of that month, the climbers ascended without problems to the North Col, but the monsoon subsequently obliged them to descend.*

*69 bottom Over the years oxygen bottles and breathing gear grew lighter and were perfected. The new models used in the mid-1930s were far better than the rudimentary equipment used by the first explorers of Everest.*

Photos: Royal Geographical Society

A sturdy group, but unlucky. From the very first days, in fact, they realized that the weather conditions on Everest were not normal. Contrary to previous years, that year the wind blew from the east, unloading a great quantity of snow. On 22nd May the monsoon had already struck Darjeeling: it swept the whole of the Indian peninsula in only four days. Shortly before that date, climbers and Sherpas had set up Camp IV at the North Col, but they soon had to descend to base camp for reasons of safety. On 3rd June, during a fresh attempt to ascend to the Col, Shipton was almost knocked down on a windy slab. It was too dangerous; they could be risking their lives. The weather was not improving, and they could only descend to base camp. And so, after a last few explorative sorties, the expedition went back down to Rongbuk.

Two years later, there was another British expedition, again on the Tibetan side. This time there was a very limited budget, equipment reduced to the essentials, but a great deal of enthusiasm. Headed by Bill Tilman, the team of climbers included top level mountaineers: Smythe, Shipton, Odell, Oliver, Warren and the young Peter Lloyd. It could also count on a group of strong, able Sherpas: Ang Tarkay, Pasang, Kusang, Tenzing and others.

On the 6th April the expedition reached

Rongbuk, after a fairly swift approach, along a more direct route than usual. Everest was in perfect conditions. In twenty days they pitched and supplied the first three high camps. But it was still too cold to climb higher, better to wait. As so, as a diversion, the group crossed Lhakpa-La and went down into the Kharta Valley, going backwards along the route followed by Mallory in 1921. In the meantime, however, the weather turned and it began to snow, and when the climbers regained Rongbuk, on 14th May, Everest had changed face. It was the prelude to another anomalous season, like that of 1936. On 18th May Camp III was again occupied. The following week Camp IV was set up on the North Col. On the 29th, Odell, Oliver, Warren and Tilman climbed along the ridge to 7,450 meters, following the young Tenzing, who was leading the way on the high snow. On the following days it continued to snow, and the group withdrew to Camp I.

In those conditions the ascent to the North Col seemed really too dangerous, and after long discussions, they decided to follow another route, passing along the main Rongbuk Glacier. In the next few days three new camps were set up, the last at 6,500 meters, just under the west slope of the North Col, which, however, did not seem any less subject to avalanches than the previous one. On 5th June they reached Camp

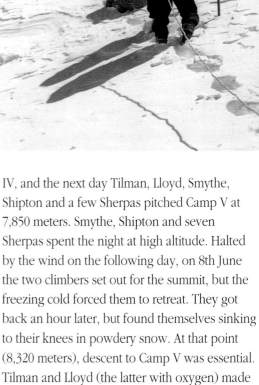

IV, and the next day Tilman, Lloyd, Smythe, Shipton and a few Sherpas pitched Camp V at 7,850 meters. Smythe, Shipton and seven Sherpas spent the night at high altitude. Halted by the wind on the following day, on 8th June the two climbers set out for the summit, but the freezing cold forced them to retreat. They got back an hour later, but found themselves sinking to their knees in powdery snow. At that point (8,320 meters), descent to Camp V was essential. Tilman and Lloyd (the latter with oxygen) made another sortie towards the Summit Ridge, but this also ended in failure. Shortly afterwards, all the climbers returned to the base camp. The last hope of scaling Everest from the north had faded. Everything had to be started from scratch. However, much time was to go by before the next attempt on the Himalayan colossus. No one knew then, but the world was shortly to be lit up by the tragic fires of a terrible war.

*70 bottom left  Animals manage to survive in the Himalayas even at fairly high altitudes, as this the group of crows photographed on the glacier at over 6,000 meters proves.*

*70 right  Bad weather and avalanches meant that for a number of days during the 1938 expedition the slopes of the North Col were impassable.*
*The expedition thus divided to search for a safe route and reached the col from both sides.*

*71 top  In the spring of 1938 the violence of the atmospheric precipitation and the intense cold (temperatures of -47°C were recorded at Camp III) slowed the climbers' progress and they were unable to proceed beyond the 8,300 meter mark.*

*71 bottom  From Camp V on Everest, at an altitude of 7,800 meters, one can look out over the East Rongbuk Glacier in a northeasterly direction.*

Photos: Royal Geographical Society

Once the last fires of the war had been extinguished, the idea of scaling Everest bloomed anew. But before the Alpine Club and the Royal Geographical Society could get the Himalayan Committee, the heir of the Everest Committee, back on its feet, a curious climbing attempt was recorded. Without a permit, Earl Denman, an engineer and self-styled climber of Canadian origin, with two Sherpas, Tenzing Norgay and Ang Dawa, entered Tibet secretly like the pundits in the good old days. They made a swift journey, without great loads, and away from the trade routes. On 8th April 1947, the little group was already at Rongbuk. Two days later, Denman, Tenzing and Ang Dawa climbed the glacier. They ascended swiftly, pitching only mobile camps, to the foot of the North Col. Then a blizzard arose and the attempt was halted just below the North Col.

That same year, the Indian subcontinent became the theatre of an important political and administrative transformation. From the ashes of the British Empire arose two different nations: the Indian Union and Muslim Pakistan. But the changeover did not take place without bloodshed. Social tensions, street fighting and bitterness between the two new nations caused millions of victims. For Westerners, part of the Himalayas became out of reach. And to the north of the great mountain chain things were even worse. Inspired by a prophecy which spoke repeatedly of imminent danger from the outside world, the Dalai Lama sealed off all Tibet's borders. Some years later it turned out that the oracle was not wrong: in the autumn of 1950, Chinese armies invaded Tibet and annexed it, later turning it into an autonomous province. The isolation of the great Tibetan high plateaus became total, and for many years no climber could cross the forbidden frontier.

In short, to all intents and purposes, the Everest adventure seemed destined to remain forever in the archives of memory. But Nepal, to everyone's surprise, opened its doors and windows to the West. In fact the presence of the Chinese armies just the other side of the Himalayas was an understandable reason for concern. On the level of international politics, the decision had various positive consequences and, obviously, immediately put the international climbing world in a hubbub. Understandably so, because the possibility of approaching Everest from the southern side revived old projects which had been set aside for some time and lit new hopes. The only initial difficulty was the very poor knowledge of the territory. Until

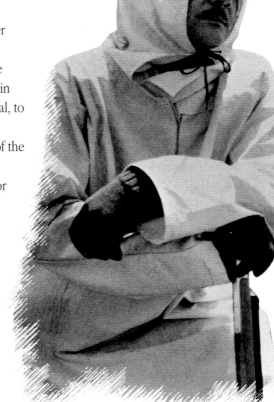

# THE POSTWAR YEARS

*72 top. In the summer of 1947 the Canadian Earl Denman, disguised as a Tibetan and accompanied by two Sherpas, surreptitiously crossed Tibet and reached the Rongbuk Glacier. He climbed as far as the foot of the North Col before a blizzard inexorably forced him back down the valley. Photo: Salkeld Collection*

*72 bottom  For climbers intending to scale Everest from the Nepalese side, the ascent route inevitably passes by way of the Khumbu Glacier which in its lower section presents a large and dangerous ice fall. Photo: Royal Geographical Society*

that moment Nepal had been an unknown land, as yet unexplored. Before thinking of scaling Everest, they therefore had to "find the mountain," exactly as had happened in the 1920s in Tibet. They had to discover the best access route to the Himalayan giant and reconnoiter the chances of an ascent on the south side.

The first expedition therefore was of a prevalently explorative nature. Compared to the past, there was a change: directing the group of explorer-climbers was an American, Charles Houston, a doctor and well-known mountaineer, who in 1936 had with Harold William Tilman led the expedition to Nanda Devi and two years later attempted to scale K2. And this was no negligible detail: in fact, Houston's presence signified the end of the British monopoly on Everest.

The expedition, of which Tilman was also a member, visited the village of the Sherpas, reached Namche Bazar, explored the Khumbu Valley and then moved on to reconnoiter the southern slopes of Everest, to the foot of the Ice Fall, the gigantic serac which gives access to the Western Cwm.

In the meantime, in London, the Himalayan Committee was planning a new attempt on Everest for autumn 1951, and gave its leadership to Shipton. Once again, however, the official attempt to scale Everest was preceded by a clandestine episode. The protagonist of this incredible adventure, which took place in the

spring of that year, was Klavs Becker Larsen, a young Dane with no climbing experience. His approach route to Everest was certainly original, as well as interesting. Together with four Sherpas, Larsen crossed Nepal and on 4th April reached Namche Bazar, where he discovered the existence of Lho-La, the passage from the Khumbu Valley to that of Rongbuk, in Tibet. With the help of eight other Sherpas, in addition to those previously engaged, Larsen attempted to cross the col, but the difficult glacier terrain drove back the party. Larsen however did not give up: he regained Namche Bazar, and took the road for Nangpa La, a col opening up west of Cho Oyu, the traditional trade route between Nepal and Tibet. On 30th April, despite the terrible weather conditions, the group reached Tibet, heading for Kyetrak. From there, thanks to a momentary lack of controls, the explorer was able to proceed undisturbed towards Lamna La and go down to Chobuk, at the lower end of the Rongbuk Valley. The route was not new—from time immemorial the traders had used it—but no Westerner till that moment had ever succeeded in passing that way. On 3rd May the party reached the Rongbuk monastery and from there took the route of the prewar British expeditions. In three days Larsen and the Sherpas reached the site of Camp III. A short rest, and on 9th May they began the ascent towards the North Col. But once again a very violent wind prevented

*73 top  From the Second World War onwards the photographs of Everest changed. It was the Nepalese side of the mountain, with the high Khumbu Valley that attracted the climbing expeditions attempting to scale the Himalayan giant.* Photo: Royal Geographical Society

*73 bottom  In the spring of 1951 the Himalayan chronicles recorded another clandestine attempt to climb the Tibetan side of the mountain, this time by the Dane K. B. Larsen. On this occasion too the attempt failed just below the North Col.* Photo: Salkeld Collection

*In the autumn of 1951, following the monsoon season, a British group completed a reconnaissance mission as far as the Khumbu Glacier. The team included: (from left to right, standing) E. E. Shipton, W. H. Murray, T. D. Bourdillon, H. Riddiford; (seated) M. P. Ward and E. P. Hillary.*

*74 center The 1951 expedition was the first to venture along the Khumbu Glacier, an area of considerable mystery, especially around the treacherous Ice Fall that made the ascent route difficult and dangerous.*

collective imagination of mountaineers and even today constitute landmarks in one of the most famous treks in the world.

At the end of September, Riddiford, Ward and Bourdillon started to explore the Ice Fall, while Shipton and Hillary climbed up the slopes of Pumori to observe the highest part of the ascent route from a suitable perspective. The idea was to climb the Ice Fall, along the Western Cwm, to reach the South Col and then move along the Southeast Ridge of Everest. The difference from the route on the Tibetan side was immediately evident: the main difficulties of the south side were above all concentrated in the first part. The first 600 meters of difference in height were an immense chaos of blocks and gigantic towers of ice. The great Khumbu Ice Fall is a river of ice affording unstable balance, as it is in continuous downhill movement. On 30th September, the first attempt to climb the Ice Fall emphasized the great dangers of the route, especially during the ascent with loads on their backs. But there were no alternatives, the ice fall was a compulsory stage.

On 4th October, Shipton, Bourdillon, Hillary, Riddiford and three Sherpas attempted to open up a way in the maze of seracs. They started out from a small camp at the foot of the great ice flow and climbed as fast as possible. At 16.00 the group was in sight of the Western Cwm, but the late hour and the excessive snowing over of the upper stretch

the ascent. Back at Rongbuk, the party learned that a Chinese official was enquiring into the presence of foreigners in Tibetan territory. To avoid arrest, Larsen immediately started back for Namche Bazar.

In the meantime, in Great Britain preparations for the autumn expedition were proceeding fast and furiously. In addition to Shipton, who accepted the appointment as head of the expedition, the group could count on Michael Phelps Ward, Thomas Duncan Bourdillon, William Hutchison Murray, Dr. Dutt, of the Geological Survey of India, and on two strong, experienced New Zealand mountaineers—Edmund Hillary and H.E. Riddiford. The Committee however excluded from the expedition René Dittert, the well-known Swiss climber proposed by the Fondation Suisse pour l'Exploration Alpine. The reason was that the Everest ascent was to be an exclusively British affair.

Like the Houston expedition of the previous year, the group set off from Jogbani, in southeast Nepal. But they were too early in the season, and the first approach stage took place in the incessant rains of the monsoon. Fortunately, in the Dudh Kosi Valley the weather improved. On 22nd September, the expedition reached Namche Bazar. Three days later, the march continued, touching on Thyangboche, Pheriche, Lobuje, the Khumbu Glacier and lastly the little lake of Gorak Shep, where the base camp was set up. These were places which were soon to enter the

forced them to retreat. It was better to try with more settled snow.

In the following days, the expedition climbers explored the surrounding mountains. Three weeks later, Shipton and his companions reascended the Pumori Ridge to get an idea of the conditions on the Western Cwm and the South Col. There was still too much snow, but they could no longer wait. It was worth making an attempt, within the limits of safety, of course. On 28th October all the climbers and three Sherpas climbed the Ice Fall and entered the Western Cwm. At a certain point towards the bottom of the hollow, two enormous crevasses barred the route. Getting round them would have required time, and Shipton ordered the party's return. It was a pity, although the way to the South Col was by now open.

In Great Britain the return of the mountaineers was greeted with great enthusiasm. The *Times* printed a special 16-page supplement with photographs, maps and Shipton's diary. In short, the Everest fever was relit, and the Committee planned a new expedition for 1952. But there was a drawback: the Swiss were stealing a march on the British, having been the first to obtain permission for an ascent from the Nepalese government. A mediation was immediately attempted, but the idea of a joint expedition quickly failed, also

*75 top  In 1952 a Swiss expedition took the place of the British team but the latter were nevertheless offered the opportunity of completing a traverse of Nup-La. The British expedition led by Eric Shipton reached an altitude of around 8,650 meters.*

*75 center  After the failed attempt on Cho Oyu, the British expedition divided into two groups, Edmund Hillary (in the photo) and George Lowe took advantage of the situation to complete the first traverse of Nup-La via the immense Gyubanare ice fall, descending by way of the East Rongbuk Glacier.*

*74 bottom  Progress amidst the seracs of the Khumbu Glacier was difficult and a route was not easy to find. The climbers picked their way through a kind of white labyrinth, amidst unstable blocks and towers moving with the flow of the glacier.*

because the Fondation Suisse pour l'Exploration Alpine had not yet forgotten Dittert's exclusion from the previous year's attempt. And so they struck a bargain: the Swiss in the spring, the British in the autumn. But even so the plan did not work. The government of Nepal decided that in 1952, Everest could be attempted only by the Swiss before and after the monsoon; on the other hand, the British could go to Cho Oyu. The Committee had no choice but to accept the decision. In any case, Shipton behaved like a gentleman and traveled to Zurich with the photographs taken during the last expedition.

*75 bottom  The British climber Alfred Gregory, a photographer and lecturer in everyday life, took part in the Shipton expedition to Cho Oyu. In 1953 he was to participate in the triumphant ascent of Everest.*

Photos: Royal Geographical Society

*76 top left In 1952 two Swiss expeditions explored the Nepalese side of Everest, one during the pre-monsoon period, the second in the autumn. This photo shows the fourth high altitude camp pitched on the Western Cwm.*

*76 top right Edouard Wyss-Dunant, the leader of the spring 1952 expedition, could count on the very best Swiss climbers and a strong group of Sherpas led by no less a figure than Tenzing Norgay.*

The Swiss group that spring was directed by E. Wyss-Dunant and gathered together some of the strongest Swiss Alpine climbers: René Dittert, Jean Jacques Asper, René Aubert, Gabriel Chevalley, Léon Flory, Ernst Hofstetter, Raymond Lambert and André Roch, who were joined by three scientists—a geologist, a botanist and an ethnologist. The team of Sherpas was led by Tenzing Norgay, now 38 years old with considerable Himalayan experience. There was excellent agreement among all the members of the expedition, and they had great mountaineering skills and much experience: it was truly impossible to ask for more. After a departure from Kathmandu, where an airport had recently been built, the group reached the base camp at Gorak Shep (5,050 meters) on 20th April, after following an approach route which was mostly new. On the following days work began on the setting up of the higher camps: the first at 5,250 meters, at the base of the Ice Fall, the second half-way up. On 30th April, the climbers reached the gigantic ice falls by going out on the left, under the steep slopes of the West Ridge of Everest, moving along a passage which was subject to ice falls. A little further on, at the approach to the Western Cwm, an enormous crevasse barred the way. They had to swiftly find a solution. The next day, with four ropes, the climbers set up a bridge to get the bearers over safely. On 6th May, Camp III was occupied, at the beginning of the Western Cwm. From there the road to the South Col turned out to be longer than foreseen, and soon two other high altitude camps were set up, the fourth and the fifth, the latter under the slopes giving access to the

South Col. On 15th May, Lambert, Tenzing, Dittert and Roch attacked the Eperon des Genevois, hindered by the oxygen equipment which was working only intermittently and badly. Two more attempts, and finally, on the 19th, Chevalley, Asper and a Sherpa reached the South Col. Shortly afterwards the route was secured with fixed ropes.

There was a pause due to a blizzard, and then the ascent recommenced. On 26th May, after a hard night bivouacking, Lambert, Flory, Aubert and Tenzing pitched Camp VI at the South Col. The following day the group attacked the Southeast Ridge and set up Camp VII—a single tent—at just under 8,400 meters. Lambert and Tenzing spent the night there and the following morning set out for the summit. But they were slow, very slow, because the oxygen apparatus was working badly. And so, on reaching 8,600 meters, a new altitude record, they turned back. A second attempt, conducted by Dittert, Asper, Chevalley, Hofstetter, Roch and five Sherpas, was halted by blizzards at the South Col.

*76 center  The great crevasse that at an altitude of 5,900 meters bars access to the Western Cwm was crossed by the Swiss climbers with a series of acrobatic roped maneuvers. Subsequently the stretch was equipped with a bridge to allow for the passage of the Sherpas with their loads.*

*76 bottom  At the bottom of the Western Cwm the ascent route followed by the Swiss climbers snaked along part of the Lhotse Face before turning towards the Eperon des Genevois.*

*77 top  As one gains altitude along the slopes of Everest the panorama over the Himalayan mountains expands. At times, having climbed beyond the layer of clouds that hangs mid-way up the mountains, one can see the highest peaks such as Makalu and Chomo-lönzo (in the photo).*

*77 bottom  Tenzing Norgay (1914-1986), the world's most famous Sherpa, began his climbing career with the British expeditions to Everest in the 1930s. In 1950 he climbed in the Karakoram. In 1951 he reached the summit of Nanda Devi. In 1952 he was employed by the two Swiss expeditions and the following year he accompanied Hillary to the summit of Everest.*

Photos: Swiss Foundation for Alpine Research.

In the autumn, there was another Swiss expedition, which included Chevalley, who directed the group, and Lambert as well as other climbers. The new arrivals were Jean Busio, Gustave Gross, Ernest Reiss, Arthur Spöhel and the American Norman G. Dyhrenfurth. Taking previous experience into account, the expedition tried to improve their equipment, starting with the oxygen apparatus. In theory, the group had good chances of reaching the summit. But many things went wrong. The weather, the precarious health of some of the climbers, and the haste factor were against them. On 31st October, on climbing towards the Eperon des Genevois, four rope parties were struck by a fall of ice. The 25-year-old Sherpa Mingma Dorje was seriously injured and died, despite Chevalley's medical treatment. The fifth and sixth camps were then set up on the Lhotse Glacier. On 19th November, Lambert, Reiss, Tenzing and seven Sherpas occupied tents on the South Col. After a very hard night, the attempt to climb the ridge failed because of the cold and wind. The expedition was over.

While the Swiss were engaged on the slopes of Everest, in Great Britain preparations for a new attempt were feverishly proceeding in the hope that the highest peak in the world would not be conquered by the Wyss-Dunant expedition. The first task of the Committee was to put together mountaineers of tested experience. But the problem was not easy to solve, because the British mountaineering world was undergoing a period of transition. The "old guard" of Himalayan climbers were by now almost all out of the running, and most of the young climbers, although able and brilliant, had never left their home rocks. The 1952 Cho Oyu expedition made it possible to select a certain number of climbers who were up to the enterprise, but the team was not enough: the group destined for Everest had to contain the best of British mountaineering. This time they could not afford to make a mistake. Even more so because in

# *T*HE YEAR OF VICTORY

*78 top  Edmund Hillary, born in New Zealand in 1919, was one of the best and toughest climbers on the Hunt expedition of 1953. During the ascent he formed a perfectly matched roped party with the Sherpa Tenzing Norgay, ascending and descending between the high altitude camps remarkably quickly.*

*78 center  John Hunt, born in 1910, a British army officer and leader of the 1953 expedition, had a wealth of Himalayan experience and great logistical skills.*

*78 bottom  The climbers from the 1953 expedition posing for a group photo together with the team of Sherpas following the "conquest" of the world's highest mountain.*

*79 top left The New Zealander George Lowe, a long-time climbing companion of Edmund Hillary, played a vital role during the final assault on the summit of Everest in the spring of 1953.*

*79 bottom left Tom Stobart, a film cameraman by profession, shot a series of high altitude panoramas. His images were to be of vital importance in presenting to the entire world the expedition's historic and remarkable mountaineering achievement.*

June 1953 the coronation of Queen Elizabeth would be held, and the "conquest" of Everest was intended to add glory to the event.

The choice of the expedition leader seemed taken for granted from the start: Eric Shipton's name was unquestioned. But slowly, within the Committee, there was a growing conviction that it was necessary to appoint alongside the great mountaineer-explorer someone to be in charge of organization. Their choice fell on Colonel John Hunt, born in 1910, a climber and member of the Alpine Club and the French Groupe de Haute Montagne. But the proposal of joint leadership did not please Shipton, who withdrew embittered.

An excellent organizer, Hunt set to work right from the first days of October 1952. His leadership had a strongly military stamp. Very rigorous, precise and filled with a great sense of responsibility, Hunt's mien was the opposite of Shipton's free, independent spirit. In any case,

Hunt immediately proved to be up to the task entrusted to him; he had very clear ideas and his schedule encountered no hitches. He knew that he had to succeed, and planned the expedition right down to the last detail, from the climbing equipment—which had to be the best the market could offer—to the oxygen equipment, which absolutely had to be used on the highest parts of the mountain. He also planned an alternative objective: Kangchenjunga—in the event that the Swiss, still engaged on Everest, should succeed in their intent.

After careful selection, the final group of climbers was composed of Charles Evans, 31, second-in-charge of the expedition and an excellent Himalayan climber; Alfred Gregory, 31, one of the best from the Cho Oyu team; Tom Bourdillon, 28, with good high altitude experience and an excellent knowledge of

*79 right Nine high altitude camps were pitched along the route followed by the British Everest expedition that climbed the Ice Fall, crossed the Western Cwm, reached the South Col and followed the Southeast Ridge.*

Photos: Royal Geographical Society

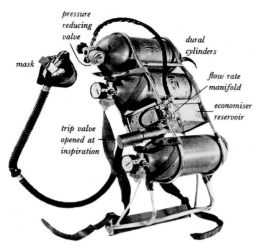

*Open-Circuit*
*Weight with 3 cylinders 41lb, with 1 cylinder 18 lb*

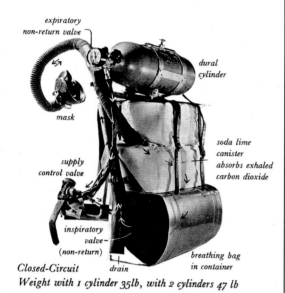

*Closed-Circuit*
*Weight with 1 cylinder 35lb, with 2 cylinders 47 lb*

oxygen equipment; the climber Michael Ward, also the doctor to the expedition. Then there were two very strong New Zealand mountaineers, George Lowe, 28, and Edmund Hillary, five years older, as well as a couple of young climbers, Mike Westmacott, 27, former president of the Oxford University Mountaineering Club, and George Band, 23, who held the same position at Cambridge University. The 34-year-old Wilfrid Noyce, a well-known climber, and officer Charles Wylie completed the team. Physiologist L.G.C. Pugh, cameraman Tom Stobart and journalist James Morris, the *Times* special correspondent, were also attached to the group.

On 8th March 1953, the expedition was at Kathmandu, where the team of Sherpas led by Tenzing Norgay was awaiting them. The departure was fixed for two days hence. In just over two weeks, the caravan reached Thyangboche. After a short rest the march continued to the camp at Gorak Shep, at the foot of Kala Pattar. But the base of the Ice Fall was still far off, and another camp was set up on the Khumbu Glacier.

The first reconnaissance began immediately. The second camp was pitched on a ledge halfway up the ice fall; the third, on 22nd April, at 6,150 meters, at the beginning of the Western Cwm. On the following days, the Western Cwm was supplied with three other camps, at 6,460, 6,700 and 7,000 meters respectively (the latter at the base of the Lhotse Face). The supply work proceeded swiftly without a hitch—food supplies, oxygen cylinders and material were heaped up in front of the tents. The two different kinds of breathing apparatus (closed circuit and open circuit) provided for the expedition were tried out. The climbers slowly began to be acclimatized. The Hillary-Tenzing rope party was very fit right from the start: it gave proof of great harmony, energy and skill. It made the ascent and descent in very short times. In the meantime, the base camp, first established at Gorak Shep, was moved forwards, onto the Khumbu Glacier, while Camp IV became the advanced operations base.

On 7th May, Hunt called the climbers together and illustrated the final plan for the ascent to the summit. The expedition leader planned for two successive attempts, with the compulsory use of oxygen after Camp V. Bourdillon and Evans, equipped with closed circuit breathing apparatus, were to open up the

*80 top  Over the course of the expedition the climbers had available 12 sets of open circuit breathing gear (those most used) and 8 closed circuit sets. Each complete set—three duralumin cylinders containing 800 liters of oxygen, tubes, taps, supply valves and mask—weighed 18.5 kilograms.*

way to the South Summit of Everest, then, if possible, attempt the main summit. At the same time, Hunt, Gregory and five Sherpas were to pitch a camp at 8,500 meters. The following day, Hillary and Tenzing were to climb to the tent with the aid of open circuit oxygen equipment, spend the night there at high altitude and then aim for the highest peak; lastly to reach the South Col.

Shortly afterwards they started to climb again. Having discarded the idea of following the Eperon des Genevois, they preferred to continue along a less direct line, along the Lhotse Glacier, to then reach the South Col with a long traverse.

The task of opening the way fell to George Lowe. On 16th May, at 7,300 meters, Lowe and Wilf Noyce mounted Camp VI. Ward subsequently took Noyce's place. Operations were, however, slowed down: there was a lot of wind and the temperatures were very low. Hunt's plan risked failure.

And so, on 20th May, accompanied by a few Sherpas, Noyce climbed back up to Camp VII with the order to reach the South Col at all costs.

The following day the British climber and the Sherpa Anullu carried out their task; immediately afterwards, on 22nd May, Hillary, Wylie, Tenzing and a team of Sherpas

established Camp VIII on the Col. Hillary and Tenzing's exploit was great; both were in top form: in less than 30 hours they climbed from Camp IV to Camp VIII to then descend for the advanced stage.

On 26th May, the final stage of the climb began. Hunt, Da Namgyal and Tenzing set out with their loads for the Southeast Ridge. But Ang Tenzing did not feel well, and his companions were forced to share the contents of his rucksack, which caused even greater fatigue.

Bourdillon and Evans attacked the ridge one hour later. Lighter, less weighted down, they overtook their companions and climbed swiftly until Evans began to have problems: his closed circuit respirator was working badly. Bent under the loads of their rucksacks, Da Namgyal and Hunt went slowly on, the leader having some trouble with the oxygen equipment. They gained some altitude but in the end were forced to stop a little above the tent pitched the year before by Lambert and Tenzing.

A little higher up, however, things began to get better. Evans's breathing apparatus finally behaved itself, and the two climbers advanced quickly. At 11.00 they reached the snowy saddle where Hunt had hoped to pitch Camp IX. Reaching the foot of the South Summit of

*81 top  All the camps established during the expedition were equipped to the highest standards thanks to the labors of the climbers and Sherpas. This was essential as the periods spent at high altitude were fairly long.*

*81 center  The food and equipment for the Sherpas and the climbers had to be carried to the base camp. In 1953 the number of porters needed to transport the loads to the camp was so great that two caravans of men had to be organized.*

*81 bottom  From Camp VII, the last prior to the South Col, the South Summit of Everest rises powerfully in the distance. The true summit, however, is over 80 meters higher.*

Everest, they moved first onto the eastern flank of the ridge, then Bourdillon followed a rocky rib with good holds. Evans again had some problems with his breathing apparatus. A zig-zag climb towards the summit cone, a stretch of deep snow and finally, at 13.00, the two climbers came out onto the South Summit of Everest. It was a record: 8,760 meters. No man, until that moment, had ever been so high. What should they do? After brief consultation, they decided on descent, but it very soon became a nightmare. Evans could hardly breathe, Bourdillon did his best to make his companion's apparatus work. And soon fatigue began to be felt. The two climbers reached the camp on the South Col literally exhausted.

The next day, Hillary and Tenzing did not manage to set out; there was too much wind. Evans, Bourdillon and Ang Temba, all in poor physical condition, set out towards Camp VII. But they did not get far: at a short distance from the tents, Bourdillon collapsed onto the snow. He was revived with oxygen, but it was clear that he could not get down without the help of a companion with some strength left. Hunt charged Lowe with the task. But this created a complication. The New Zealand climber was essential for the final stage of the ascent. In the end the expedition leader thought it over and himself accompanied Bourdillon, Evans and Ang Temba down.

On the morning of 28th May, the final "assault" began. Lowe, Gregory and Ang Nyima set out first, laden with food supplies and equipment. Later, Hillary and Tenzing attacked the ridge, following in their companions' footsteps. The two groups met up near the old Swiss tent and went on together to the place where the material left by Hunt and Da Namgyal lay. The party shared out the loads—23 kilos each, except for Hillary, who carried 5 kilos more on his back than the others—and took up

the climb. At 8,500 meters, the team halted. It was 14.30. Lowe, Gregory and the Sherpas went back down; Hillary and Tenzing prepared for the night. The slope on which they pitched the tent was not ideal, but they had no choice but to make the best of it. After having supper and drinking a large quantity of liquids, to prevent dehydration, inside the tent Hillary opened the valve of an oxygen cylinder. By 3.00 the cylinder was empty, but it didn't seem to be a problem; they had to start drinking again—essential at high altitudes—and prepare breakfast. At 6.30, Hillary and Tenzing were ready to depart. Gloves, down-filled anoraks, windjackets, boots, oxygen masks and cylinders, they looked like caricatures of extraterrestrials.

The first part of the climb was hard work because of the crusty snow which broke under the climbers' weight, making them sink to their knees. Higher up Hillary and Tenzing found the cylinders left by Hunt and Bourdillon. Fortunately they were not completely empty. They would be useful on their return. At the foot of the South Summit, the New Zealander decided to climb directly up along the slope. The snow was definitely unstable, but he went

*82 left Hillary and Tenzing paused to rest at Camp IV. To recover from the fatigue of the ascent and to rehydrate their bodies after a prolonged period at high altitude they drank liters of hot tea.*

*82-83 Secured to a safety rope, Wilfred Noyce carefully crosses a metal ladder over a great crevasse slashed deep into the ice of the Western Cwm.*

*82 bottom Hillary and Tenzing painstakingly checking their equipment in view of the final assault on the summit of Everest concluded on the 29th of May 1953.*

*83 top The Sherpa Tenzing Norgay leading the roped party with ice axe and crampons along the steep, icy slope descending from Lhotse. They were heading for Camp VIII at the South Col.*

*83 bottom The most important phase of the British expedition of 1953 is about to begin: Edmund Hillary and Tenzing Norgay depart for the final push to the summit of Everest.*

Photos: Royal Geographical Society

ahead just the same, followed by Tenzing. At 9.00, the two climbers were at the top of the South Summit. Then they went along the Summit Ridge, which had enormous cornices sticking out eastwards. It was impossible to follow the line of the earlier assault: for safety reasons they had to keep to the opposite side. Luckily the snow held well. At a certain point the rope party reached the base of a rocky pillar (the Hillary Step). The New Zealander climbed the pillar, using the chimney technique, exploiting the space between the rock and the delicate cornice of ice. Tenzing followed on his heels. Higher up the ridge the inclination decreased and progress became gradually easier, so that the climbers could proceed side by side. A hump of ice, another and yet another. Lastly the snowy dome of the summit and, all around, nothing else, only lines stretching downwards, and emptiness. It was 11.30 on 29th May. On one side they could discern the East Rongbuk Glacier; far away, thousands of meters lower down, the colors of the Tibetan high plateau stood out, almost a mirage in that world white with ice and snow. A few minutes later, Hillary looked towards the North Ridge, and remembered Mallory and

Irvine; instinctively he sought a sign, an object, evidence of their passing. He found nothing, of course. Crouching in the snow, Tenzing prepared offerings for the gods of Chomolungma.

A few biscuits, just a bite to eat, and a few minutes later it was already time to descend: the limited reserve supplies of oxygen obliged them

to remain within their scheduled times.

One hour later, Hillary and Tenzing were on the South Summit, but did not stop. Lower down, they loaded the cylinders left by Evans and Bourdillon on their backs. At the tent at Camp IX, they changed cylinders, picked up their personal belongings and continued on their way down. In the vicinity of the South Col,

*84 top left  Hillary and Tenzing tackling the final part of the route to the summit of Everest. With their mittens, down-filled jackets, and oxygen masks they looked like beings from another world.*

*84 top right  Hillary climbing the Southeast Ridge with oxygen breathing equipment. This was the last phase of the climb. At 9.00 the 29th of May, Hillary and Tenzing reached the top of the South Summit, two and a half hours later they set foot on the true summit of Everest.*

*84 bottom  Hillary and Tenzing about to leave the South Col. That day they pitched Camp IX below the South Summit of Everest, the last outpost prior to the final assault on the summit.*

*85 top left  Edmund Hillary and Tenzing climbing roped together and equipped with breathing gear towards the Southeast Ridge. Behind them rises the Lhotse Face.*

George Lowe climbed up to meet the two with hot soup and new cylinders. A questioning glance and Hillary shouted "Hey, George, we knocked the bastard off."

At Camp IV, the rest of the expedition was oblivious to their triumph. The arranged signal from the South Col was not visible due to fog. The wait was highly emotional. Jim Morris, the *Times* correspondent, and the cameraman Tom Stobart were the ones who let the whole world know the outcome of the final attempt. The meeting with their companions was an explosion of joy. Morris hung on Hillary's every word, made him talk, noted down everything and was the first to descend, accompanied by Westmacott. Once at base camp, he sent a Sherpa to Namche Bazar with a message in code which, apparently, said the exact opposite of what had happened. This was understandable: correspondents of rival newspapers were in ambush. The Namche radio operator transmitted the signal to the British ambassador in Kathmandu, who in turn immediately informed the *Times.* The editorial staff correctly interpreted the message and, on the morning of the coronation of Queen Elizabeth, 2nd June, the London paper came out with the exclusive news headline. Other articles appeared on following days. And one month later, the paper returned to the subject with a 32-page supplement entitled "The first ascent of Mount Everest."

*85 top right  Charles Evans, the second in command of the 1953 expedition, reached the South Summit of Everest (8,765 meters) using closed circuit breathing gear.*

*85 bottom  Tenzing Norgay celebrating on the summit of Everest. It was just after 11.30 on 29th of May 1953, an historic day for Himalayan climbing.*
*A brief rest and a few minutes later it was time to descend: the restricted reserves of oxygen obliged the climbers to return as soon as possible.*
Photos: Royal Geographical Society.

Hillary and Tenzing's climb concluded an important chapter in the history of Everest but, as will soon be realized, was in no way the conclusion of the history of its climbing. In fact, as was true for other Himalayan mountains, the first ascent triggered many other ascensions and an endless number of attempts. Even the interval between the first and the second scaling of Everest was much shorter than one might expect: only three years. And it is curious to reveal that, despite the ambitions which converged on Chomolungma from many sides, the second ascent was made by a Swiss expedition, led by Albert Eggler. And it was an important ascent, although less "sensational" than the previous one, because the climbers, as well as repeating the way led by Hillary and Tenzing, also managed to set foot on the summit of Lhotse.

Two years later the resumption of climbing activity was also reported on the north side. But

# $B$UT THE STORY CONTINUES

it was almost impossible, for the moment, to understand what was happening. After the Chinese invasion of Tibet, in the autumn of 1950, everything that happened beyond the Himalayan curtain was unknown to the Western world. But yet something was going on. In 1958 a Sino-Soviet reconnaissance party was reported to be on the North Face of Everest and then, two years later, the news spread of a Chinese ascent. For the time being the news which reached the West from the New China Agency was so fragmentary that it was difficult to make head or tail of it. Official communiqués referred to a very large expedition, headed by Shih Chan-chun, but the writing of the Chinese reports was decidedly obscure and did not help in understanding how the ascent was carried out. The heights of the first camps on the East Rongbuk Glacier coincided with those of the British prewar attempts.

The ascent times, however, were strange. But so it is: the report was so sparing in details that any guesswork is vain. Party slogans instead of schedules, inclinations and altitudes, political propaganda instead of technical notes. In the days of the Cultural Revolution, the classical ascent accounts at times took on strange forms: this is a fact. In the midst of this confusion, however, the names of the climber Hsu Ching (in the first stage of the ascent) and the climbers who made up the rope party to the summit

*86 bottom left  A rope party of the great Chinese expedition that, in the May of 1960, reached the summit of Everest, is ascending a section of the glacial route equipped with fixed ropes and signaled with flags. The fairly large expedition could count on a continuous turnover of the teams of porters stocking the high altitude camps.*
Photo: Chinese Mountaineering Association

*86 top left  Shih Chan-chun was the leader of the 1960 Chinese expedition that reached the summit after having climbed to the North Col and followed the North and Northeast Ridges.*
Photo: Salkeld Collection

*86 top right  According to the official dispatches, Gonpa, the Tibetan climber who formed part of the rope party that climbed to the summit, led the last part of the climb that concluded in the night.*
Photo: Salkeld Collection

*86 center Wang Fu-chou, roped together with his companions Chu Yin-hua and the Tibetan Gonpa (all three used oxygen breathing gear), reached the summit of Chomolungma at 4.40 in the morning on the 25th of May, following a 19-hour climb.*
Photo: Salkeld Collection

*86 bottom right Chu Yin-hua, a member of the Chinese 1960 expedition, was the last to arrive at the summit but it is difficult to extract much detail about his precise role during the ascent from the contemporary report.*
Photo: Salkeld Collection

*87 top Teams of climbers ascending along the Rongbuk Glacier. The altitudes of the first camps below the North Col coincide with those of the pre-war British attempts. The climbing times, on the other hand, are imprecise.*
Photo: Chinese Mountaineering Association

*87 bottom A rope party taking a moment's rest during the climb on the North Face. The information provided by the New China Agency spoke of a camp pitched at 7,200 meters. Little or nothing is known about the next section up to an altitude of 8,500 meters where the climbers pitched another camp.*
Photo: Chinese Mountaineering Association

repeatedly appear: Wang Fu-chou, Chu Yin-hua, a Tibetan named Gonpa and Liu Lien-man (who, however, at a certain point gave up the ascent). We also know that, after pitching a camp at the North Col, the climbers set up fixed tents at 7,200 meters. We know little of what happened in the stage immediately above this, except that, at 8,500 meters, the climbers set up another camp. The Chinese route went along the ridge line (according to Mallory's old plan). The report however did not include any mention of the First Step, while the adventuresome climb of the following one is reported, with a description of a human pyramid. In the end, after a very long night climb with the help of oxygen, without being able to eat or drink for many hours, the Chinese rope party reached the summit of Everest at 4.40 on 25th May 1960, leaving on the summit dome a flag and bust of Mao Tse-Tung. Needless to say there is no photographic documentation of the arrival at the summit.

Many conjectures have been made about the undertaking, and it is truly difficult, 27 years later, to express opinions on the subject. Especially because during the period in which these events took place conditions in China were light years away from those in the Western world. However, the few photographs taken of the ascent were studied carefully as well as a few details visible in a sequence filmed by Chu Yin-hua at high altitude, and these seem to correspond perfectly to reality. In particular, according to veteran British climbers, one of the pictures may have been taken just above the Second Step, at about 8,700 meters.

Spring 1963: the Americans were back on Everest. The leader of the expedition, Norman G. Dyhrenfurth, 45, mountaineer, Himalayan expert of fame, explorer and writer, knew the area well. He had taken part in the Swiss post-monsoon attempt of 1952 and had gone back to the area in 1955 for an attempt on Lhotse. The very large group of climbers included Allen C. Auten, Barry C. Bishop, John E. Breitenbach, James Barry Corbet, David L. Dingman, Daniel E. Doody, Richard M. Emerson, Thomas F. Hornbein, Luther G. Jerstad, James Lester, Maynard M. Miller, Richard Pownall, Barry W. Prather, Gilbert Roberts, William E. Siri (the expedition doctor), William F. Unsoeld, James W. Whittaker and an Englishman, Colonel Jimmy Roberts.

At first Dyhrenfurth's plan was to climb along the Southeast Ridge (the route of the first ascent) and descend by the West Ridge, thus inaugurating the first traverse of the Himalayan giant. But Hornbein shortly afterwards proposed a different idea. The West Ridge had never been explored, why, therefore should they tackle it on the descent,

20th February and one month later set up the base camp. The first part of the route was the same for them all up to the Western Cwm and the first obstacle to be overcome, as always, was the Ice Fall. To hasten the search for a route through the maze of seracs and crevasses, Dyhrenfurth climbed up along the slopes of Lho-La and, by means of walkie talkies, indicated to the group led by Unsoeld the way to follow. During the second ascent attempt, the sudden collapse of a wall of ice caused the death of Breitenbach. It was the first serious accident on the Ice Fall. The group's spirits sank, and some even wanted to leave the expedition. But the ascent went on. On 2nd April, at 6,500 meters, in a hollow of the Western Cwm, Camp II was set up, soon to turn into the advance camp. From this point on, the two groups in the expedition attempted different routes: the first headed for the Lhotse wall, aiming for the South Col, the other planned to cross the Western Cwm leftwards, reaching the west shoulder of Everest and then to climb the West Ridge.

Face of Everest, although the terrain might in parts turn out to be dangerous. In particular, Hornbein had his eyes on a snow gully (today known as the "Hornbein Couloir") which makes it possible to get round the most difficult part of the ridge. The next day, at 7,650 meters, Bishop, Hornbein and Unsoeld selected the place to pitch a new camp.

On 13th April, the group returned to base camp with clearer ideas. But Dyhrenfurth decided to speed up operations on the normal route to the South Col: the successful outcome of the expedition was becoming pressing. Faced with the need to reach the summit at all costs, the West Ridge group hesitated. Hornbein and Unsoeld risked remaining isolated, but fortunately Corbet and Emerson, by now quite acclimatized, decided in favor of the new route. And it did not matter that almost all the porters were engaged on the high camps on the normal route. Hornbein and his companions put in action an experimental winch which made it possible to lighten the work.

In the meantime the climbers engaged on the

# THE FIRST TRAVERSE OF EVEREST

at the limit of their strength? It was better to attempt it on the ascent, and then go down along the way which leads back to the South Col. Among the climbers in the group, however, there were some who were interested exclusively in reaching the summit by the shortest, easiest route, "Big Jim" Whittaker, for example. During the approach march, the climbers in the expedition divided into two factions: Hornbein, Unsoeld, Bishop, Breitenbach, Corbet, Dingman and Emerson, all excellent rock climbers, wanted especially to attempt the West Ridge. Dyhrenfurth, Whittaker, Siri, Jerstad, Pownall and Gilbert Roberts, more keen on snow and ice mountaineering, were instead for an ascent from the South Col. The others reserved judgment. The only mediator between the two groups, Willi Unsoeld, was aware that the difference of goals might have negative consequences on the undertaking of the ascent.

The expedition set out from Kathmandu on

In theory, the second plan ought to have had priority over the ascent on the normal route. And so, on 3rd April, Unsoeld and Bishop explored the first part of the new itinerary. Two days later, Bishop and Hornbein pushed on to 7,150 meters, sufficiently high to realize that, at least up till the West Shoulder, the route did not pose great problems. On the 7th a provisional camp was pitched at the beginning of the traverse. But the tent was soon taken down and, just under the West Ridge, at 7,200 meters, Camp IIIW (W standing for West) was established. On the following morning, Hornbein, Bishop, Unsoeld and Dingman climbed to the shoulder. Suddenly they found themselves suspended over two different worlds: on the one side, the Western Cwm, on the other the Rongbuk Glacier. Above them, first snow-covered, then rocky and sharp, rose the West Ridge. In case of excessive difficulty, the climbers thought they could climb to the left of the ridge, on the North

*88 left  The American expedition of 1963 worked toward two separate objectives: the first was a repetition of the route opened in 1953 by Hillary and Tenzing passing by way of the South Col and continuing along the Southeast Ridge, the second objective was an ascent along the West Ridge. Bishop and Unsoeld, victims of frostbite in their extremities, are seen in this photo at the base camp while waiting to return to Kathmandu for treatment.*

*88 right  The weather was not always favorable in the spring of 1963. The Americans frequently had to cope with blizzards and storms and the plan to climb the West Ridge risked being abandoned.*

*89  Not all the climbers on the American expedition were satisfied with a repetition: some of them (Hornbein, Bishop, Unsoeld, Dingman and others) aimed to climb the West Ridge. A new route was about to be opened.*

Photos: National Geographic Society

classical itinerary proceeded swiftly. On 29th April, Whittaker, Dyhrenfurth, Gombu, Ang Dawa and a little group of support Sherpas mounted a camp (the fifth) on the South Col and the following day pitched another at 8,365 meters on the Southeast Ridge. Then on 1st May, the departure for the summit began. Dyhrenfurth and Ang Dawa gave up almost immediately; Whittaker and Gombu, who were fitter, succeeded in reaching the summit of Everest.

On the following days the supporting rope parties were not able to repeat the ascent: at Camp VI there was no more oxygen and, before attempting the summit again, they needed to arrange a supply of new cylinders. In the meantime Dingman, Prather and several Sherpas, who had

decided to attempt Lhotse, were forced to withdraw. The days which followed were dedicated to rest. Once at base camp, however, they noticed that the oxygen supplies were very limited, and a lively argument arose. In any case, plans were soon being made once more. The idea was to set up two more attempts simultaneously, one to the West Ridge and the other along the normal route, with the meeting of the two rope parties at the summit and a common descent towards the South Col. Corbet and Emerson immediately set the winch working and began to supply Camp IIIW. On 15th May, Hornbein, Unsoeld and a few Sherpas set up the fourth camp at 7,650 meters. The next day they continued on the way, but

during the night a furious snowstorm swept ridges and slopes, and it was a miracle that the three tents of Camp IV did not plunge downhill.

On 20th May the fourth camp was repaired. The following morning the ascent continued. Hornbein and Unsoeld spent the night at 8,300 meters, in the little tent at Camp V, pitched some hours earlier. It was still dark when the American rope party set out for the summit. They tackled the limestone ridges of the Yellow Band, where the Hornbein Couloir barely opens the way. A little higher up, the two Americans climbed a very difficult, brittle wall. Just one more rope length, and they were at 8,500 meters. Higher up, the ascent path turned right and finally followed the

West Ridge to the summit slopes. At 18.15, Hornbein and Unsoeld finally reached the summit, where they found the American flag planted by Whittaker twenty-one days before. Twenty minutes later, they started the descent towards the South Col. The two climbers reached the South Summit in the last light of the day and continued in the dark. At one point they heard voices below them. It was Jerstad and Bishop who, having climbed up the normal way, had reached the summit of Everest during the afternoon and were now going slowly down. Hornbein and Unsoeld joined their fellow climbers, who very close to total exhaustion, and encouraged them to carry on. But it was useless; they were forced to bivouac. The night never seemed to pass, the cold biting into their flesh. At dawn, Dingman and a Sherpa climbed up to look for their companions, all of whom fortunately had survived. Some hours later, at the advance base, the first traverse of Everest was concluded.

*91 top  May 1st, 1963: The Sherpa Nawang Gombu raises the expedition flags on the summit of Everest. Together with Whittaker he had just completed a repetition of the original route.*

*91 bottom  An American climber crossing a crevasse with a metal ladder. Climbing techniques had evolved by the 1960s but in certain situations the systems used by the pioneers were still valid.*

Photos: National Geographic Society

*90-91  At 18.15 on the 22nd of May, 1963, Tom Hornbein and Willi Unsoeld completed their new route and reached the summit where they found the American flag planted by James Whittaker earlier that month.*

Before and after the American expedition, Everest was also attempted by Indian climbers, who in those years were achieving a certain amount of fame on the Himalayan mountains. The Indian Mountaineering Foundation, set up in 1958, aimed above all at scaling the highest peaks in Asia. Everest was naturally the greatest dream for the young climbers who had made a national hero of Tenzing Norgay, the Nepalese Sherpa who had been living for many years in Darjeeling. The first Indian expeditions, in 1960 and 1962, succeeded in climbing only to the foot of the South Summit of Everest. The third attempt was more successful: in May 1965, after pitching a camp at 8,500 meters on the Southeast Ridge, in three climbs, between 19th and 29th May, as many as nine mountaineers reached the summit. A few months later, Nepal again closed its frontiers; and for three years, from 1966 to spring 1969, Everest remained an impossible dream. When the Khumbu Valley route again became available, the mountaineers by then had other plans. The long ascent up the classical

South Col route and the Southeast Ridge were no longer enough, they wanted more. Himalayan mountaineering started to fall under the spell of the great face walls. New ideas and incredible rock ascents on all sides shook the foundations of the climbing world, leaving a strong mark on the younger generations. The desire to move forwards, to take a different road was felt everywhere. And so why not in the Himalayas?

The beginning of a new mountaineering chapter on the highest peaks in the world dates from the early 1970s. And the event which inaugurated the change—the first ascent of the gigantic South Face of Annapurna by a British expedition—was truly extraordinary. It was an enormous step forward: a sign that major Himalayan climbing was about to abandon the easiest, most logical ways in order to tackle the great faces, along routes which were as direct and continuous as possible.

This was also true of Everest: first the most outstanding peaks, then the walls. And the first of

# $\mathcal{T}$HE EPIC OF THE SOUTHWEST FACE

these to draw the climbers' attention was the massive wall which looks southwest: a formidable face which towers 2,400 meters above the Western Cwm—first with steep snow slopes; then, higher up, with a great rock face. In the middle of the face is a great snow field, which from afar looks like a gully and which rises to meet the Yellow Band at about 7,900 meters. But instead of ending there, the icy couloir divides into two branches and takes on a "Y" shape: on the right it rises towards the Southeast Ridge; on the other side, it bends towards a narrow ledge which winds among the rock towards the right and (although this is not at all clear from below) goes to join the great Upper Snowfield.

The first to be granted permission to climb the wall, with three consecutive expeditions, were the Japanese, who had by now been gaining familiarity with the Himalayan peaks for some years. The first reconnaissance party to the Southwest Face was in autumn 1968: a quick glance at the "problem," without going above 6,500 meters. One year later the Japanese climbers returned with more serious intentions. Having set up base camp and an advance camp on the Western Cwm, in October

they pitched other tents at 7,000 meters (Camp III) and 7,500 meters (Camp IV), the latter at the foot of the Central Couloir, and a fifth camp at 7,800 meters. The novelty was that, because of the thinness of the snow cover, unlike all the previous expeditions, above a certain altitude (around 7,500 meters) the various camps could only be pitched with the help of metal platforms acting as a base. On 31st October, a rope party made up of Naomi Uemura and Masatsugu Konishi explored the left ledge of the Central Couloir, convinced that this was the right way to reach gain the Upper Snowfield. The following day, Hiroshi Nakajima and Shigeru Satoh continued the ascent for a stretch. The ascent line seemed to be promising, but they did not push further on.

As punctual as clockwork, the Japanese climbers returned to Everest in the spring with a large, new expedition, accompanied by an independent group which was planning to ski down from the "roof of the world." As well as the Southwest Face, the climbing team counted on repeating the normal South Col route. The main group, led by Saburo Matsukata, numbered 39

climbers (including a woman, Sekuto Watanabe). If we add to these the Sherpas and the 33 members of the skiing group, it is immediately clear that the first part of the ascent stretch, the same for them all, could only be "busy." And the Ice Fall and the first part of the Western Cwm, as may easily be guessed, do not tolerate crowding. So much so that at the beginning of April, six Sherpas in the ski group were buried under an avalanche, and a few days later another high altitude porter was the victim of a falling serac. But their problems did not end here, because shortly afterwards, at Camp I, a sudden heart attack seized Kujoshi Narita, the youngest climber in the expedition. It was a hard blow for everyone, and progress seemed bound to halt. But they went ahead just the same. The expedition leader cancelled the plan to climb the face and asked the climbers to concentrate their efforts on the normal route. Not everyone agreed, however, and the Southwest Face was again discussed. In short, the climbers resumed both programs.

On 11th May, Uemura and Terup Matsura reached the summit from the classical South Col

route; the next day Katsutoshi Hirabayashi and the Sherpa Chotare also succeeded in the ascent. At the same time, the group engaged on the face encountered great difficulties: the snow was very thin, the establishment of the camps demanded great precautions, progress was more difficult than foreseen and the dangers due to rock falls increased day by day. Slowly, the first rope parties climbed above 8,000 meters and came in sight of the ledge which made it possible to surmount the Yellow Band. But the passage turned out to be in bad condition, and in the end was not even attempted: it would be left for another time. On 21st May, all the mountaineers returned to base.

In the camp the Japanese morale was high: two weeks previously the ski group had accomplished its goal. Yuichiro Miura had successfully skied down from the South Col towards the foot of the Lhotse wall, reaching a speed of over 150 k.p.h. Madness, considering the altitude, the brake system (a parachute) and the conclusion of the slide. But luckily everything went well and, after a bad fall, the skier had managed to stop just before a huge crevasse.

94-95 *The great Khumbu Ice Fall, a chaotic mass of seracs and deep crevasses, is an obligatory passage for those heading for the Western Cwm. Here the equipment requires constant maintenance due to the frequent avalanches and the continual movement of the glacial masses.*

94 bottom *The Japanese climber, Naomi Uemura, who during the 1970 expedition climbed in partnership with another Japanese, Reizo Ito, was one of the most active climbers of the group tackling the Southwest Face.*

95 bottom This photo shows some of the protagonists of the international expedition of 1971. From left to right can be recognized P. Mazeaud, J. Evans (the coordinator of the group that attempted the Southwest Face), N. Dyrenfurth (the expedition leader), M. and Y. Vaucher and C. Mauri.

95 top Norman G. Dyhrenfurth, the leader and organizer of the international expedition of 1971, was an Everest veteran. He took part in the second Swiss attempt of 1952, participated in the expedition to Lhotse in 1955 and led the American group in 1963.

Photos by John Cleare/ Mountain Camera

The following year, the Ice Fall and Western Cwm rang with the voices of another party of mountaineers. It was a large international expedition led by Norman Dyhrenfurth, including well-known climbers from various countries, an entire BBC television team, a journalist and a geologist. Italy was represented by Carlo Mauri; France by Pierre Mazeaud; Great Britain by Dougal Haston and Don Whillans, as well as by the doctor-climber Peter Steele; Switzerland by Michel and Yvette Vaucher; West Germany by Tony Hiebeler; Austria by Wolfgang Axt and Leo Schlömmer; India by Harsh Bahaguna; Japan by Reizo Ito and Naomi Uemura. But there were also the Americans Duane Blume, David Isles, Gary Colliver, John Evans and Dr. David Peterson. Then the Norwegians, Jon Teigland and Odd Eliassen. And lastly Colonel Jimmy Roberts, second-in-charge of the expedition. Their twofold objective: the West Ridge and the Southwest Face. On paper, the group had all the cards needed to conclude two fine undertakings. Instead, the expedition turned out to be a parade of stars in constant argument, and the international amalgamation was a disaster. All the members wanted to shine and no one was willing to stand aside in the interests of the final outcome. Due to linguistic and cultural affinities, from the first days, two groups formed spontaneously within the expedition: the Anglo Saxons and the "Latins." The former in particular aimed at the Southwest Face; the second was concerned with a direct route along the West Ridge.

The first part of the route, the same for everyone, did not pose excessive problems. On 5th April Camp II was set up at 6,580 meters, at the beginning of the Western Cwm. Then the two groups split up. Evans, Whillans, Haston, Hiebeler, Colliver, Ito, Uemura, Peterson and Schlömmer attacked the face; Axt, Teigland, Eliassen, Mauri, Mazeaud, Bahaguna, Steele, Yvette and Michel Vaucher tackled the West Ridge.

Conditions on the face were excellent; the way up the West Ridge, on the other hand, was unsatisfactory. In any case, on both routes a first high camp was pitched (in reality the third from the Ice Fall base). But not everything went well, and the first conflicts soon began, especially concerning supplies. But there was worse: on 18th April, hoping to avoid a blizzard which was blowing at high altitude, Harsh Bahaguna and Wolfgang Axt decided to descend towards Camp II. In a traverse stretch, the Indian climber slipped and was left hanging from a fixed rope, unable to free himself, at the mercy of wind and cold. Axt climbed down to seek help, and rescue operations began immediately. But the wind hindered recovery operations, and despite the efforts of his companions, Bahaguna died of cold and exhaustion.

The expedition morale was zero. Hiebeler returned to Germany. What could they do? The West Ridge group completely disintegrated. Mazeaud and Mauri and the two Vauchers asked

96-97 The team of
Sherpas working hard
on the Ice Fall to supply
the camps of the
international expedition
pitched on two different
routes: the South Col and
the Southwest Face.

96 bottom The Briton D.
Whillans and the
Austrian L. Schlömmer
(photo taken at Camp III)
were, together with D.
Haston, J. Evans, G.
Colliver, R. Ito, N. Uemura
and D. Peterson,
members of the group that
attempted the Southwest
Face.

*97 top After a number of days of constant blizzards, Camp II, pitched at an altitude of 6,580 meters at the beginning of the Western Cwm, resembles an abandoned polar outpost.*

*97 bottom Ian Howell of the BBC, reassures the director of the television team, Anthony Thomas, during the crossing of crevasses in the Ice Fall at an altitude of 8,500 meters.*

*Photos by John Cleare/ Mountain Camera*

Dyhrenfurth if they could climb along the normal route. They voted, the Southeast Ridge plan was approved and the expedition leader agreed. But very soon problems began again. The supply of the higher camps was slow: the difficulties of the initial stretch cannot be taken lightly. Almost every day the Ice Fall route had to be re-secured due to its movements, and the organization of transport turned out to be difficult, since the porters, once they reached the Western Cwm, had to follow different paths to keep both groups happy. At a certain point, Jimmy Roberts, in charge of camp supplies, suggested to Dyhrenfurth that they should concentrate efforts on a single objective, the Southwest Face. They voted. The majority agreed, but Michel and Yvette Vaucher could not express their opinions because they

route, with the help of the Ito-Uemura rope party. On 5th May they occupied Camp V, at 7,925 meters. Then they moved leftwards, to have a look at the previous Japanese attempt. Too steep. So they attempted to ascend vertically. No go. Lastly they tried to climb on the right side of the face. They pitched a tent at 8,290 meters (Camp VI) and took shelter to await better weather, determined to make an all-out attempt. To avoid descending, they economized as much as they could on oxygen, using it only at night. Behind them, apart from the Japanese and some Sherpas, the route was deserted. Schlömmer offered his help in exchange for the leadership of the rope party. The British refused, but perhaps they really needed a change of the guard. A new argument arose. Shortly afterwards, above Camp VI,

were not present. Mazeaud did not agree, he felt deceived and taken in and descended with Mauri to base camp. In the hours which followed, explosive arguments broke out. Dyhrenfurth was accused of bias. Someone said there was a plot, and everything ended in a big row. In the end, the South Col group abandoned the expedition. The Southwest Face team, on the other hand, did not give up. In the meantime the expedition leader fell ill and Jimmy Roberts took his place.

Engaged at high altitude, Whillans and Haston were more than ever determined to complete the

Whillans and Haston noticed that their path was moving towards the Southeast Ridge. They were tired and the temptation to cross in that direction was strong but, after the disagreements with Mazeaud and his companions, it was essential to finish the route in the logical manner. The stretch above them, a chimney, was beyond their strength. They consulted each other. Rather than take the easy way out, they preferred to give up.

The failure of the Dyhrenfurth expedition seemed like a warning: no more over-populated expeditions and more care in the choice of

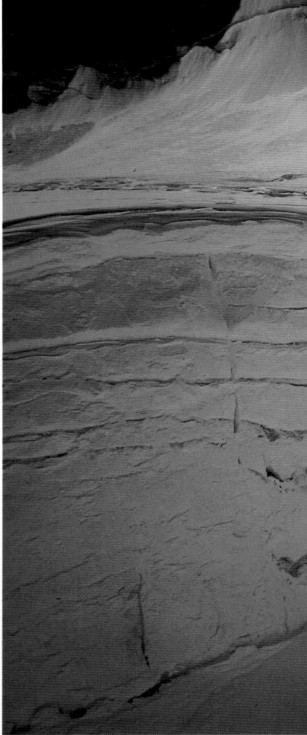

98 A team of Sherpas from the autumn 1972 expedition descending the Ice Fall as quickly as possible after completing the labor of transporting materials to the high altitude camps. In the sections where the route passed beneath the ice pinnacles any delay could be fatal.
Photo by Ken Wilson/ Chris Bonington Library

98-99 A group of climbers and Sherpas from the Bonington expedition to the Southwest Face crossing a gigantic crevasse cutting deep into the Western Cwm.
Photo by Chris Bonington/ Chris Bonington Library

participants. It seems clear that after the unhappy experience of 1971, a radical change in perspective might have been expected. But things continued in the same way. In the spring of 1972, the face was assaulted by another group which had the same features as the previous one. With one essential difference. Whereas Dyhrenfurth's ideas had been inspired by supranational ideals, the international expedition put together by Dr. Karl Maria Herrligkoffer seemed to be governed above all by financial motives: famous participants and different nationalities mean more sponsors, more newspaper coverage, more television, and hence more money.

Herrligkoffer aimed high; he wanted the best. He invited the pick of German and British mountaineers, but they did not all accept. Chris

Bonington, for one, refused. In the end, the expedition was made up of Austrian climbers, except for the Britishers Doug Scott, Don Whillans and Hamish MacInnes, the Italian Leo Breitenberger and the Swiss Hans Berger, as well as of a cameraman and three scientists.

As was predictable, from the start Herrligkoffer's climbing campaign ran into constant problems, even some serious ones. The man in charge of base camp returned to Europe due to problems of acclimatization. Horst Vitt, 32 years old, died of a lung edema on his arrival at Gorak Shep. Then a quarrel broke out among the Sherpas about insufficient equipment. Lastly, the rivalry between the German-speaking climbers and the British halted collaboration at a high altitude—to the point that the British preferred to pack up and leave. And this was the end: on 18th

May the Austrian team reached the site of Camp VI and continued towards the highest point reached by Haston and Whillans the previous year. But despite their efforts, they could not proceed, and the group was forced to return to base camp.

A few months later, in the autumn of 1972, a new attempt was made. The face was attacked by a seasoned British expedition led by Chris Bonington, who gathered around him the pick of British Himalayan climbers, all highly experienced mountaineers: Mick Burke, Nick Estcourt, Dougal Haston, Hamish MacInnes, Doug Scott, Kelvin Kent, Graham Tiso, David Bathgate, Tony Tighe and Dr. Barney Rosedale, and, as usual, Jimmy Roberts.

The first part of the ascent was carried out impeccably. Despite a few problems with the weather, on 30th September Camp II was set up (advance base) and preparations for Camp III

*99 right The Southwest Face of Everest is a formidable sheer wall rising 2,400 meters above the Western Cwm. The initial slopes are steep and snow-covered but higher up there is a great rock wall with an icy Y-shaped corridor.*
Photo by Keiichi Yamada/Chris Bonington Library

*99 bottom Camp II at the start of the Western Cwm, represented an advance base for the 1972 British expedition and was vital in that it guaranteed supplies for the climbers tackling the Southwest Face.*
Photo by Ken Wilson/ Chris Bonington Library

*100 left  Rather than the high temperatures of the middle of the day it is above all the constant movement of the glacier down the valley that provokes the collapses that are such a feature of the immense glacial expanse of the Ice Fall. This photo shows the men of the 1972 British expedition tackling an apparently simple section.*

*100 top right  The ice bridge represents the only natural means of crossing the deep crevasse that plunges to the bottom of the Western Cwm. Due precautions need to be taken before venturing onto it.*

*100 bottom right There are moments during the blizzards in which everything disappears, swallowed up by the furious, unrelenting wind and great swirls of snow. At times, after days of bad weather the tents housing the Bonington expedition were buried if not damaged by the thick snow.*

were begun two days later. On 12th October, Haston and MacInnes had already begun to set up the way to Camp V. But time was short, and soon the terrible winter wind began to blow. The tents were flung about madly, threatening to tear. In the whirlwind, Camp IV was continuously hit by fragments of ice and stones, which seemed to have the tents as their target. The expedition was paralyzed and the idea of descending seemed to be gaining ground. Luckily, at the beginning of November, things began to get better. All the tents were again occupied, and work was begun on preparing Camp VI. The aim was to continue the route attempted in 1971, but the chimney discovered by Whillans and Haston was not climbable: the wind had swept away all the snow. They could only give up.

A few days later, when the expedition seemed destined only for the archives, a serious accident occurred. During the descent, Tony Tighe, intent on climbing up the Ice Fall, disappeared into the maze of seracs, probably knocked down by a fall.

*101  Some sections of the Ice Fall, the immense series of seracs on the Khumbu Glacier, are composed of chaotic masses of ice pinnacles of all sizes, precariously leaning against each other.*

Photos by Doug Scott

*102 top  The expedition of Japanese women led by Eiko Hisano posing for a group photo. The group was made even more numerous by the presence of the Sherpas and a Japanese television team.*
Photo: Japanese Ladies Climbing Club

*102 center  In the spring of 1975 a Chinese expedition led by Shih Chan-chu reached the summit by way of the North Col. A Tibetan woman named Phanthog and 8 other climbers reached the top of Chomolungma.*
Photo: Salkeld Collection

Autumn 1973 brought a new attempt on the face. After a spring ascent by the Monzino expedition, which covered the normal route with a truly excessive use of men and means (in their retinue there were even two Italian military helicopters), at the end of the monsoon another climbing group of considerable dimensions arrived on Everest: a team of 48 Japanese climbers and 33 Sherpas led by Michio Yuasa. Part of the expedition followed the route of the previous year but could not go higher than 8,300 meters; the other, on 26th October, reached the summit from the South Col. It was the first post-monsoon ascent of Everest in the history of climbing, but it cost Yasuo Kato and Hisahi Ishiguro a hard night's bivouac during the descent, and some severe frostbite.

The chapter of the Southwest ascent ended only two years later, in the autumn of 1975. But before and after the summer monsoon in 1974, two other ascent attempts were recorded: the first along the normal route, by a Spanish expedition led by Lorente Zigaza: the second on the West Ridge, directed by the Frenchman Gérard Devouassoux who, together with five Sherpas, died in an avalanche. Then, in the

*102 bottom  On the 16th of May 1975, the 35-year-old Japanese climber Junko Tabei reached the summit of Everest after having climbed along the classic Nepalese route with the Sherpa Ang Tsering. She was the first woman to set foot on the top of Everest.*
Photo: Japanese Ladies Climbing Club

spring of 1975, two other important events deserve mention: the first ascent of Everest by a woman (concluded on 16th May by the 35-year-old Japanese Junko Tabei, with the Sherpa Ang Tsering) and the Chinese ascent (documented this time) of the North Ridge, with nine climbers, including a Tibetan woman named Phanthog, reaching the summit.

102-103 *In the autumn of 1975 a British expedition led by Chris Bonington finally succeeded in conquering the Southwest Face of Everest, the formidable* wall of rock and ice on which numerous attempts had previously come to grief. Photo by Adams/ Image Bank

But let us go back to the ascent of the Southwest Face, which was achieved by Chris Bonington and his faithful band, "old" (44) Hamish MacInnes, Doug Scott, Dougal Haston, Mick Burke, Nick Estcourt, Martin Boysen, and Mike Thompson, as well as Paul Braithwaite, Allen Fyffe, Ronnie Richards, Dave Clarke, Pete Boardman and Mike Rhodes, the latter from the climbing club of Barclays International Bank, which financed the expedition. Also taking part in the expedition were Adrian Gordon, in charge of the advance camp, Drs. Jim Duff and Charles Clarke, four BBC correspondents and a journalist from the *Sunday Times*.

The first problem that Bonington had to deal with was how to avoid wasting too much time in transporting food supplies and material to the base camp so that the face could be attacked immediately after the monsoon. So, to hurry up operations, before the summer monsoon set in, the expedition leader had had a depot set up near Namche Bazar. Secondly, before attacking the face he had to study the route thoroughly. In other words, he had to answer one fundamental question: was it better to follow the previous attempts step by step, or to take up the old 1971 Japanese plan?

The British expedition installed their base camp on 22nd August. In the meantime Estcourt and Haston, who had gone ahead of the group, were already at work on the Ice Fall. On 2nd September, Camp II, the so-called "advance base," was already able to receive the climbers. Higher up, the tents were not pitched in the usual places, but more protected spots were found, even though lower down. In short, everything proceeded very swiftly and without hitches. On 11th September, the fourth camp was occupied and, less than one week later, Bonington and Richards pitched the next one, checked supplies, and fixed ropes. They then had to come to terms with the Yellow Band and the narrow snow gully, but above all with the ledge already attempted by the Japanese, a very difficult, delicate stretch, with a problematic rope length. In the end, after a hard struggle, Estcourt and Braithwaite succeeded and came out on the Upper Snowfield. The problem of the Yellow Band

104 top  Located to the side of the great gully that cuts into the lower part of the Southwest Face, the British expedition's Camp IV was protected with impermeable canvas sheets (clearly visible in the photo) to prevent the powder snow from infiltrating between the slope and the box tents.

104 bottom
Mike Thompson and Dougal Haston resting at Camp VI, the highest on the Southwest Face of Everest at 8,300 meters, pitched above the "Ramp."

104-105  The Sherpa Ang Phurba anchors Dougal Haston with a rope in the section of the interminable Southwest Face of Everest that begins from the exit of the snow-filled gully at an altitude of over 8,200 meters

was finally resolved and the way to the summit should no longer present other surprises.

On 22nd September, just above the passage of the ledge, Haston and Scott set up Camp VI. The next day they continued to climb and secured 500 meters with fixed ropes. Then, on the morning of the 24th, they set out for the summit, determined to bivouac at high altitude if circumstances should require it. It was 3.30. At the first light of dawn they were already at the end of the fixed ropes. They climbed swiftly, but a problem with Haston's breathing apparatus stopped them for an hour. At 15.00, after much difficulty—soft snow on unstable

slopes of 60°—they reached the South Summit of Everest. There was still the final stretch of the Southeast Ridge. Three hours later, Haston and Scott were treading the snow on the summit and photographed each other beside the tripod along with the red flag left there by the Chinese in the spring. But it was late, there was little daylight left. And so they started the descent. Again the ridge, the Hillary Step and lastly the South Summit, where they bivouacked. The altimeter showed 8,760 meters: no one, till then, had ever spent the night at such an altitude. They dug a hollow and tried to warm themselves as well as they

105 bottom  Mick Burke, mountaineer and cameraman, was one of the leading climbers on the Bonington expedition to the Southwest Face of Everest. He was seen for the last time on the 26th of September, just below the summit, but then disappeared without trace.

Photos by Doug Scott

*106-107 September 24th 1975: after having scaled the Southwest Face the British climbers Dougal Haston—a few steps from the summit where the tripod with the red flag left by the Chinese expedition of the previous spring can be seen—and Doug Scott reached the summit of Everest.*

could. The oxygen cylinders were empty, and it was bitterly cold. But they could do nothing, just wait for the dawn. And then the hallucinations began. Haston had a lively argument with an imaginary companion. Scott talked to his boots. Scenes from another world.

In the morning, at the first light of day, the summit rope party set out and at 9.00 was already at Camp VI. Fortunately, the bivouac without oxygen had not harmed the two climbers. That same day, Boardman, Boysen, Burke and the Sherpa Pertemba settled into Camp VI, ready for the second attempt. On the following morning, the group set out for

the summit. Boysen had trouble with his breathing apparatus, then lost a crampon and lagged behind. In the end he gave up and went back to the tent. Boardman and Pertemba continued the ascent. At 11.00 they reached the South Summit, two hours later the summit. The weather was getting worse. The Englishman and the Sherpa set out on the descent, and a little further down met Burke, determined to get to the summit. The two British climbers agreed to meet each other lower down, on the South Summit. But Burke did not make the appointment. In the meantime the weather was steadily worsening

106 bottom Dougal Haston posing for a photo taken in the evening light by his companion on the summit of Everest. During the descent, caught out by the failing light, the pair bivouacked on the South Summit of Everest.

107 top Doug Scott, having reached the summit with Haston, also wanted his souvenir snap-shot alongside the Chinese tripod. Their stay at the summit lasted but a few moments, however: it was 16.30 and they had to descend as quickly as possible.

107 bottom The British climber Dougal Haston, armed with an ice axe and crampons, intent on scaling the Hillary Step.

Photos by Doug Scott

and visibility was rapidly decreasing. What to do? At 16.30 Boardman and Pertemba decided to descend: they did not feel up to bivouacking in that weather.

Facts proved them right, the descent turned out to be not at all easy. The Sherpa slowed down his pace and the snowstorm increased in intensity. Boardman had the impression they were on the wrong path. At 19.30 the adventure finally ended. But there was an unexpected sequel. The blizzard nailed Boysen, Boardman and Pertemba to Camp VI (Burke was never found). Thirty hours later, the final descent was a true liberation.

108  The original
objective of the expedition
led by Wolfgang Nairz
in 1978 was the South
Pillar, but the climbers
subsequently fell back
on the better known route
from the South Col and
along the Southeast Ridge.
This photo shows the
Eperon des Genevois and
the flank of Lhotse.

108-109  Camp III of the
Austrian Everest
expedition was located
on the Lhotse Face and
represented the point of
departure for access to
the South Col.

The ascent of the Southwest Face of Everest truly ended an epoch. Almost as if it had freed itself of an obsession, the world of Himalayan climbing could finally observe the giant mountain between Nepal and Tibet in a more relaxed manner, and perhaps also dream of some new route or different ways of reaching the summit.

So, in the spring of 1977 seven New Zealanders and a Canadian, led by Keith Woodford, attempted to go it alone and tackled the normal Nepalese route without the help of Sherpas. The expedition did not succeed in reaching the summit, but all the climbers got to 7,500 meters, and two of them pushed on to the South Col, before being driven back down by the wind. It was a demonstration that it is possible to reach high altitudes even with few means, without the organization of unwieldy

# THE YEARS OF CHANGES AND NOVELTY

national expeditions. In short, an important sign of change, above all in a traditional milieu such as that of Himalayan climbing.

It was no coincidence that just one year later, Reinhold Messner and Peter Habeler, believers in an anti-technological climbing method, came on the scene ready to experiment on Everest. They were convinced that they could ascend like the prewar Himalayan pioneers, and amidst general skepticism, planned an ascent without oxygen. An important wager, and with an outcome that could not be taken for granted. But it was not so simple to obtain permission to climb, because the Nepalese government was assailed by too many requests. The two climbers therefore joined the Austrian expedition led by Wolfgang Nairz, on the understanding that they would be able to move independently.

The preparation of the South Col route was fairly swift, and Messner and Habeler actively helped in the establishment of the high camps. They were both very fit, and Nairz decided to give priority to the attempt without oxygen. And so, on 23rd April, the two set out from Camp III.

*109 top  The second camp pitched by the Austrian expedition was located in the Western Cwm. It was also used as reference point by Reinhold Messner and Peter Habeler who joined the expedition in order to make an attempt on Everest without using oxygen.*

*109 center  An Austrian climber from the expedition led by Wolfgang Nairz in the spring of 1978, climbing along a fixed rope towards the South Col where Camp IV had been pitched.*

*109 bottom  One of the Austrian climbers can be seen here heading from the South Col to Camp V at an altitude of 8,300 meters. This was the last shelter before the final pitch to the summit.*

Photos: Archive Wolfgang Nairz

*110-111 Horst Bergmann, climbing in a roped party, follows in the footsteps of his companions along a snowy slope at an altitude of 8,600 meters. In spite of the use of breathing gear, the altitude slows progress.*

During the night, however, Habeler felt ill and was forced to re-descend: the sardines of the night before had made him ill. Messner decided to go on alone. He climbed to the South Col with two Sherpas and pitched Camp IV, but a terrible blizzard halted him for two nights. The situation was becoming perilous, but fortunately on the morning of the third day the bad weather changed and the three men succeeded in descending. A few days later, the rest of the expedition started out. On 3rd May, Nairz, Robert Schauer, Horst Bergmann and the Sherpa

Ang Phu reached the summit with oxygen cylinders; and the ascent was later repeated by Reinhard Karl and Oswald Ölz.

At the base camp, Messner and Habeler re-examined the situation calmly. In the end, their doubts overcome, they left Camp III for the South Col. With them were the English cameraman Eric Jones and three Sherpas. They all climbed without oxygen, but the equipment nevertheless included a couple of cylinders in case of dangerous situations. On the morning of 8th May, Messner and Habeler started out from

the South Col camp. They carried only light rucksacks. They sank into the soft snow, and reached Camp V. From there they continued to climb unroped because, in those conditions, they had no chance of managing any worthwhile form of belaying. Just under the South Summit, Habeler removed his rucksack. On the Summit Ridge, full of eastward-jutting cornices, the two climbers decided to rope up. They, however, proceeded together, which is not at all easy at that altitude, because mental sharpness and promptness of reflexes are often not up to par, unless a breathing apparatus is used. At 13.00, the rope party finally reached the summit. It was an important moment in the history of Himalayan climbing, a true step forward. But right then, Messner and Habeler had no time to think about their achievement. They would discuss it later, perhaps at the base camp.

An embrace, a few seconds of emotion, the ritual photograph. Messner lingered a little on the

their lives. The little group faced the snowstorm and began to descend to where they found the fixed ropes which helped them to reach Camp III, where the expedition doctor awaited them. Three hours later, the group continued to descend to the advance base camp, and safety. A few days later the news of the ascent without oxygen had flown round the world.

The 1970s had other surprises in store. Towards the end of the decade, those following Himalayan affairs had new reason to be excited by the Everest story. The objective in that period, the most evident goal, was the long West Ridge in its entirety. The American 1963 route had excluded all of its first part, and in the higher stretch, by deviating on the North Face along the Hornbein Couloir, had left unsolved the question of a direct ascent. In 1974, a French expedition led by Gérard Devouassoux (whose name we have already mentioned) had attempted to climb it, cutting out Lho-La from

*111 left Two climbers from the Nairz expedition ascending the last section of the classic Nepalese route to the top of Everest: they are at an altitude of around 8,700 meters, that is to say, almost at the height of the South Summit.*

*111 top right Wolfgang Nairz posing for his souvenir photo at the summit. The Austrian climber offered Reinhold Messner and Peter Habeler the logistic support of his expedition so that they could test the possibility of climbing to the summit of Everest without using oxygen bottles.*

*111 bottom right May 3rd, 1978: Horst Bergmann has just reached the summit of Everest. Robert Schauer, Wolfgang Nairz and the Sherpa Ang Phu also climbed with him, all using oxygen.*

Photos: Archive Wolfgang Nairz

*110 bottom Reinhold Messner and Peter Habeler reached the summit of Everest without the aid of oxygen at 1.00 on the 8th of May. Messner is struggling to return to the tent while suffering from painful ophthalmia. He had frequently removed his sunglasses to film with a small video camera and soon paid the price.*

summit calotte; Habeler instead began to descend: he was worried. One hour later he was already at the Col, miraculously unhurt after a dangerous slip. Eric Jones went to meet him and guided him to the tent. Messner arrived an hour and a half later. He was almost blind: he had often removed his dark glasses to film with a small telecamera, and ophthalmia had soon affected him. That night a terrible blizzard arose. Messner was moaning from the pain in his eyes, but categorically refused oxygen. The following morning, they had to descend at all costs, to save

the itinerary for political reasons. But nothing had come of it because of bad weather: after the setting up of Camp III at 6,950 meters, a backlash of the monsoon had unloaded heavy snowfalls on the ridge. And, soon after, on the evening of 9th September, between the two camps an enormous avalanche had detached itself; the movement of air had destroyed all the lower tents and caused a further snow slip, which had ended up right on the tents of Camp II. The final casualty list of the disaster was heavy: six dead (five Sherpas and the expedition leader).

No new attempt was made on the West Ridge until 1979, when a large group of Yugoslavian climbers (mostly from Slovenia), all mountaineers of great technical skill, directed by Tone Skarja, attacked the Nepalese side of Lho-La. Having set up base camp at 5,350 meters on the Khumbu Glacier at the end of March, the expedition started out immediately to secure the way towards the Col, protecting it from a chaotic fall of seracs. The first stretch of the route, which rose on rock to the left of Lho-La, had passages up to the V degree. To speed up the transport of loads to Camp I, just to the left of the Col a winch was set up. In the meantime, the peak rope parties began to secure the ridge which, above Lho-La, has an inclination up to 55° and level IV stretches. On 14th April, Camp II (6,770 meters) was ready to hold 12 climbers; four days later a third camp

at 7,170 meters was pitched, under the West Shoulder of Everest. Further up, the ridge became easy up to Camp IV, or 7,520 meters (this last stretch was also climbed by the Americans in 1963, but they deviated onto the North Face). On 9th May, after an interlude of bad weather, the Slav climbers pitched Camp V (8,120 meters), the last outpost before the summit. The following day, Viktor Groselj and Marjan Manfreda set out for a first attempt, but the difficulties of the way (one stretch had up to V-degree passages), the intense cold and some problems with the breathing apparatus stopped the two-person rope at 8,300 meters. Two days later, Dusan Podbevsek and Roman Robas tried, but they got only a little higher than their companions. Lastly, on 3rd May, the final attempt, by Jernej Zaplotnik, Andrej and Marko Stremfelj. There was a lot of wind and the thermometer showed -35°C. Shortly afterwards Marko Stremfelj gave up—the valve of his breathing apparatus was not working; the other two continued without problems. Higher up they climbed past a stretch of difficult rock—a V-degree length and two others of IV. Lastly they again picked up the Americans' route and, ten minutes before 14.00, they reached the summit. On the way down, the two climbers followed the Hornbein Couloir, and in the late evening reached Camp IV.

Two days later, Stane Belak, Stipe Bozic and the Sherpa Ang Phu repeated the ascent, but on the way down were forced to bivouac in the Hornbein Couloir, at approximately 8,200 meters. The following morning, the three who had reached the summit were joined by their companions from Camp V. Despite the hard bivouacking, Belak and his companions seemed able to continue the descent independently. But they were tired. So much so that Ang Phu slipped and did not have the strength to stop his fall. His body was found the following day, 1,800 meters further down.

*112 top  In the spring of 1979, Tone Skarja led a group of talented Slovenian climbers to the West Ridge. The expedition pitched a base camp at 5,350 meters on the Khumbu Glacier and then attacked the Nepalese face of Lho-La,* *the col from which the ridge departs. The long ridge which decends westward from the summit of Everest, sharply divides the North Face (in the photo). Overlooking Tibet from the Nepalese side and the Western Cwm.*

*112 bottom  One of the Slovenian climbers ascending towards the West Shoulder. In the background is the powerful bulk of the Everest pyramid: the route to the summit is still long and hard.*

*113 top  Tone Skarja, the expedition leader.*

*113 bottom  The arrival at the summit after an ascent lasting many days came as an enormous relief. The route had demanded the scaling of particularly difficult sections, some at high altitude, and to make matters worse the breathing gear acted up.*

Photos by Tone Skarja

*112-113  Here two Slovenian climbers can be seen ascending the western side of the West Shoulder of Everest with the aid of fixed ropes.*

*A short distance away, at an altitude of 7,170 meters, the third high altitude camp had been pitched.*

*Long and demanding, the West Ridge is one of the most beautiful and logical routes to the summit of Everest.*

*The American route of 1963 avoided the whole of the first section and on the upper reaches turned towards the Hornbein Couloir.*

The 1970s marked a considerable step forward in the field of Himalayan climbing, but the following decade was no less outstanding. Immediately taking up activity on the slopes of Everest was a Polish expedition led by Andrzej Zawada and made up of climbers whose names would soon be well known. On 17th February 1980, after a cold, windy period, Leszek Cichy and Krzysztof Wielicki set out from the South Col in the early hours of the morning and reached the summit at 14.00. It was the first winter ascent of Everest. A great demonstration of stamina and tenacity, achieved in difficult weather conditions.

In spring, Zawada's group was again on Everest, with its eyes on the South Pillar. The previous group, however, was joined by climbers of the calibre of Jerzy Kukuczka, Wojciech Wroz and Andrzej Czok, who proved

Shigehiro, two climbers in the same expedition, concluded (without oxygen supplies on the last stretch of the climb) a new direct route on the right-hand side of the North Face, with a final stretch picking up the Hornbein Couloir. Reaching the summit at 16.30 on 10th May, the Japanese rope party was forced on the descent to make a bivouac in harsh conditions without oxygen. It reached Camp V just before midday the following day with no damage. The new route had required the setting up of a base camp on the central Rongbuk Glacier, a long stretch of fixed ropes and five high altitude camps.

Shortly afterwards, in August, Reinhold Messner returned to Everest. The South Tyrolean climber did not want to miss the opportunity of a "first" strike on the North Face, which had been attempted by the British before the war. After some weeks of acclimatization,

solo, without using oxygen and carrying his tent in his rucksack, he climbed from base camp to advance camp at 6,500 meters. On 18th August, he set out early in the morning for the North Col. He reached it two hours later, despite a fall into a crevasse which he fortunately managed to get out of. From there, without stopping, he climbed higher and bivouacked at 7,800 meters. The following morning he crossed the North Face of Everest to reach the Great Couloir, the gully in which Norton had climbed above 8,500 meters in 1924. At approximately 8,200 meters to the left of the couloir, he stopped to bivouac. Lastly, on 20th August, carrying with him his ice-axe and a camera, he completed the way along the couloir, reaching the Northeast Ridge and carried on doggedly towards the summit. It was the first solo ascent of Everest, without oxygen

# A MEMORABLE DECADE
## (1980-1990)

immediately to be equal to the situation. The ascent technique was the usual one, with five high altitude camps, the use of oxygen and long stretches of fixed ropes. Starting out at 8,300 meters from Camp V, on 19th March Kukuczka and Czok reached the summit of Everest. They had finished their oxygen supply on the South Summit, but did not have serious problems. They regained the tent of the last camp during the night, after an uninterrupted haul of 17 hours. The new route, the seventh on the mountain and the shortest on the south side, had technical difficulties ranging from the III to the IV degree on rock and snow slopes with an inclination of 55°.

In the same period, on the North Face a Japanese expedition was active. China had shortly before opened its frontiers to foreign climbers, and the Japanese were among the first to take advantage of the event. The result was that on 3rd May, Yasuo Kato reached the summit of Chomolungma after having climbed the last stretch of the Northeast Ridge alone. He was the first climber to boast an ascent on both sides of the "roof of the world."

One week later, Takashi Osaki and Tsuneoh

*114 left  Returning from the summit of Everest, two members of the Polish expedition of 1980 (Andrzej Czok and Jerzy Kukuczka—Jurek to his friends), snapped a souvenir photo for their album. A few years on they were to become famous, especially Kukuczka.*

*114 right  In the spring of 1980 the extremely strong Polish expedition led by Andrzej Zawada opened a new route in the Nepalese side of Everest (seen in this photo) that ascended along the South Pillar.*

and along a new route. This time it was truly a breakthrough for Himalayan climbing.

In the autumn of 1981, an American expedition led by John B. West, as well as conducting an important schedule of scientific research, traced a variant to the classical route on the South Col. One year later, thanks to a group of Russian climbers, a truly grandiose new route took shape. The route stretched along the Southwest Face of Everest (more precisely, on the pillar left of the great central depression in the face wall) and came out on the West Ridge at a height slightly above 8,500 meters. The USSR team, 17 climbers in all, was led by Evgeny Tamm and made use of a vanguard entrusted with the task of perfectly securing the Ice Fall. From the base of the face, the Soviets set up five high altitude camps. The first four, at respectively 6,500, 7,250, 7,850 and

8,250 meters, were pitched from 25 March to 22 April. The last was pitched after a particularly difficult stretch. After some days of rest, on 3rd May Eduard Myslovsky and Vladimir Balyberdin established Camp V at 8,500 meters, less than 50 meters from the West Ridge. The following day, the rope party reached the summit in the early afternoon. Balyberdin did not use oxygen. At 22.25, Sergei Bershov and Mikhail Turkevich in their turn reached the summit of Everest. Both rope parties redescended to Camp V at 6.00 the next day. That same day, 5th May, Valentin Ivanov and Sergei Yephimov climbed to the summit; and three days later the ascent was repeated by Kazbek Valiev and Valeri Khrishchaty. Lastly, on 9th May, it was the turn of Yuri Golodov, Vladimir Puchkov and Valery Khomutov. A great team success on a route of high technical difficulty.

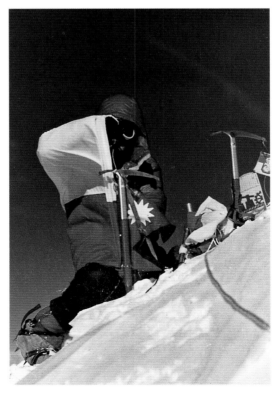

115 top  The last light of day lingers on the top of the mountain as a member of the Polish expedition struggles against the cold and the difficult terrain. The expedition led by Zawada succeeded in completing on the 17th of February the first winter ascent of Everest.

115 center left  The Polish winter expedition of 1979-1980 had to fight against intense cold and extremely violent winds. A test of stamina and tenacity.

115 center right The Polish spring expedition united at base camp for the classic group photo. The team put together by Andrzej Zawada, universally recognized as a great organizer, was composed of excellent climbers accustomed to operating in very severe atmospheric conditions.

115 bottom. The climber Andrzej Czok is immortalized on the summit of Everest by Jerzy Kukuczka on the 19th of May 1980. At that time little was known in western mountaineering circles about the Polish climbers and their ascents.

Photos by Andrzej Zawada

In the same period, a small British expedition led by Chris Bonington attempted the Northeast Ridge in Alpine style and without using oxygen. Everything went well up to 8,300 meters. Pete Boardman and Joe Tasker, two of the best British Himalayan climbers at that time, were sighted up to the base of the Second Pinnacle. Then they disappeared, probably betrayed by a cornice which protrudes onto the East Face. Searches brought no result. But in the spring of 1992, on the Rongbuk side, at 8,200 meters, a Russian/Japanese expedition was to come across the body of Boardman.

The disappearance of the two well-known British climbers made a great impression. The loss was serious, but, as always, the great wheel of climbing continued to turn. For a year, on Everest, a new "question" had been coming to a head: the gigantic East Face, still unexplored. A formidable icy wall, jutting over the Kangshung Glacier between the Northeast and Southeast Ridges. In 1921 George Mallory had given an impressive description of it.

After a first reconnaissance in the autumn of 1980, exactly one year later an ascent attempt was recorded. Led by Louis Reichardt and Richard Blum, the expedition included well-known climbers, such as John Roskelley, Gary Bocarde, David Breashears, George Lowe, Chris Jones, and Kurt Diemberger as cameraman. The group set up an advance camp and two high altitude camps, secured two kilometers of fixed ropes and overcame great technical difficulties. On 4th October, however, it was halted at 6,750 meters due to the strong danger of avalanches.

*116 left Al Burgess climbing along the Eperon des Genevois to join the classic Nepalese route that runs along the Southeast Ridge of Everest.*

*116 top right A climber from the 1982 Canadian expedition climbing the pitch separating the second and third high altitude camps between the Western Cwm and the Lhotse Face.*

*116 center right October, 1982: the Sherpas Lhakpa Tsering and Pema Dorje, in the service of the Canadian expedition led by William March, climbing the summit crest of Everest. Behind them rises the South Summit.*

*116 bottom right The two Sherpas who climbed to the summit of Everest with Pat Morrow captured by their climbing partner's camera.*

*117 October 7th, 1982: the Sherpas Lhakpa Tsering and Pema Dorje are closing in on the summit. Not far away is Pat Morrow, the Canadian climber who took the photo.*

Photos by Pat Morrow

118-119 A mountaineer from the American expedition of 1983 climbing solo along the sheer ridge that plunges to the Kangshung Glacier. One false move could cost him his life.
Photo by Andrew C. Harvard

118 bottom The climber Kim Momb allows himself a brief pause before tackling the last stretch to the summit. After having gained the Southeast Ridge on the 8th of October, Momb, Buhler, and Reichardt reached the summit of Everest via a new route.
Photo by Louis F. Reichardt

*119 top  The American climber George Lowe, attempting the East Face of Everest with the expedition led by James Morrissey, at work on the gigantic spur at the center of the Kangshung Glacier.*
Photo by
Chris Kopczynski

*119 center  David Cheesmond attempting to scale a sheer wall on the difficult central spur of the East Face. The climber can count on the presence of the old fixed ropes left by the American expedition of 1981.*
Photo by
Andrew C. Harvard

*119 bottom
On the summit of Everest Carlos Buhler cannot resist lifting his arms in triumph. This moment marked the conclusion of his team's climb along the eastern side of Everest.*
Photo by
Louis F. Reichardt

The Americans came back to the attack in 1983, led this time by James Morrissey. The new expedition was made up of Carlos Buhler, Kim Momb, Louis Reichardt, Jay Cassell, George Lowe, Daniel Reid, John Boyle, David Cheesmond, David Coombs, Andrew Harvard, Christopher Kopczynski, Geoffrey and Carl Tobin. At the center of the East Face, they took the main line of the great Spur—1,200 meters of unstable rock and ice—which in 1981 had caused great difficulties and demanded long preparatory work. Exploiting in part the fixed ropes which were still in good condition, they set up the first camps and then, with the aid of a small motor-driven winch, proceeded to transport the loads. The last camp was set up on 25th September, at 7,860 meters. The weather was fine and settled. On the morning of 8th October, Buhler, Momb and Reichardt set out for the summit. Sinking in the deep snow, after six hours of effort, they reached the Southeast Ridge at 8,470 meters. At 14.30 the rope party was at the summit. Shortly afterwards it was time to descend. Faster than his companions, Momb succeeded in reaching Camp I that evening. Buhler and Reichardt, who were more tired, stopped at Camp III and the following morning were accompanied down by Kopczynski. That same day, Cassell, Lowe and Reid repeated the ascent.

A few months later, the Japanese conducted their second winter ascent. The first, in December 1982, had cost the lives of Yasuo Kato and Toshiaki Kobayashi (only Kato, however, had reached the summit on that occasion).

In the years which followed, repeated climbs were recorded (almost all along the normal route), many attempts and some outstanding ascents. In the autumn of 1984, for example, an Australian expedition succeeded in climbing the entire Great Couloir without oxygen, using four high altitude camps (the last at 8,150 meters). On 3rd October, Greg Mortimer and Tim Macartney-

Snape reached the summit, while another member of the expedition, Andy Henderson, was forced to descend 50 meters before attaining the summit, because it was so late.

A few days later, Phil Ershler, member of an American expedition led by Louis Whittaker, completed another partially new route which, from the Northeast Ridge, crosses the North Face of Everest at 7,300 meters and ends by coming out into the Great Couloir. On 20th October, Ershler set off from a camp at 8,100 meters with John Roskelley, who, however, gave up at 8,500 meters, and in the afternoon reached the summit without oxygen.

In the summer of 1986, the Swiss climbers Jean Troillet and Erhard Loretan amazed the climbing world with a very swift ascent on the North Face. Accompanied by the French climber Pierre Béghin to 8,000 meters, the two first took the 1980 Japanese route (with some variation). They climbed the whole night, continuing also

which the 1983 route ran, and comes out near the South Col, to then continue to the summit along the Southeast Ridge. On 12th May, Stephen Venables reached the summit alone: slower, Webster and Anderson gave up near the South Summit. None of them made use of oxygen. The route was repeated in 1992 by a Chilean expedition.

Over that same period (spring 1988), Himalayan news reports recorded a double traverse (north–south and south–north) of Everest by a gigantic expedition (283 people in all, half of them at the base on the north side and the other half on the Nepalese side), organized by the Chinese Mountaineering Association, Japanese Alpine Club and Nepal Mountaineering Association. At 9.30 on 5th May, after climbing the Northeast Ridge, the Sherpa Ang Lhakpa, the Japanese Noboru Yamada and the Tibetan Tserin Dorje reached the summit. An hour later, by way of the South

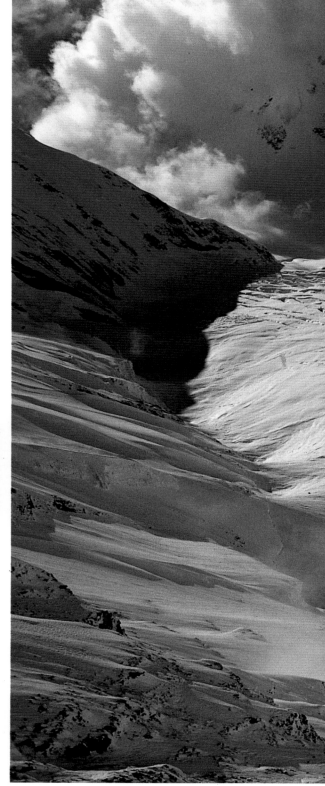

the next morning. A 10-hour rest, and at 21.00 they attacked the Hornbein Couloir. Four more hours of climbing and they stopped to wait for the dawn. They reached the summit in the early afternoon of 31st August. Their descent was very fast: with long slides, in only five hours they reached the base of the face. A true exploit: less than two days for the ascent and descent!

Spring 1988: on the East Face another great route was born. Credit for the undertaking is due to an international expedition led by the American Robert Anderson, and made up of his fellow American Edward Webster, the Canadian Paul Teare and the Englishman Stephen Venables. With three high altitude camps, the new route passes left of the great spur along

*120 top In the autumn of 1984 and Australian team succeeded in completing the entire length of the Great Couloir on the North Face of Everest without using oxygen. The climber Geoff Bartram reaches an altitude of 7,000 meters along the White Limbo route. Behind him can be seen the imposing ice-capped peak of Changtse and the North Col.*
Photo by Lincoln Hall

*120 bottom  This photo shows two members of the Australian expedition, Lincoln Hall and Tim Macartney-Snape at the end of their descent.* Photo by Colin Monteath/ Hedgehog House

*120-121  Greg Mortimer arrives at the ice cave of Camp II at 6,900 meters. At the bottom, deep in the abyss, can be seen the principal stream of the Rongbuk Glacier.* Photo by Colin Monteath/ Hedgehog House

*121 bottom  This photo shows a climber ascending the Great Couloir along the White Limbo route. It was the first time that a new route was opened to the summit of Everest without the use of breathing gear. The photo was taken at an altitude of around 7,500 meters.* Photo by Lincoln Hall

Col, the Sherpa Ang Phurba (whose oxygen cylinders had been empty for two hours) and the Chinese Ringen Puncog and Da Tsering also reached the top. Twenty minutes later, Ang Phurba began to descend along the Northeast Ridge, beginning the traverse. An hour afterwards, Ang Lhakpa followed him, though heading down the Nepalese side. Shortly before 13.00, a team from Japanese television arrived to film the meeting at the summit, which was broadcast live to the world. The climbers left on the peak then set off downward to carry out the double traverse. The same day, three more climbers (one Nepalese, one Japanese, and one Chinese) reached the summit from the Northeast Ridge and returned along the same route as they had ascended. Finally, on 10th May, two more climbers from the same expedition made it up to the summit from the South Col.

*122 top The Sherpa Pertemba (on his third ascent to the summit of Everest) and the British climber Chris Bonington slowly scaling the icy slopes below the South Summit.*
Photo: Chris Bonington Picture Library

*122 center April, 1985: Chris Bonington, who joined the Norwegian expedition led by Arne Naess, reached the summit with a number of companions along the classic Nepalese route. Between the 21st and 30th of April the expedition succeeded in taking 9 climbers and 8 Sherpas to the summit of Everest.*
Photo: Chris Bonington Picture Library

In the autumn of the same year, assisted by a support team and exploiting the traces of other expeditions, the Frenchman Marc Batard completed a fast ascent on the normal Nepalese route. The chronometer recorded 22 hours, 29 minutes for the ascent, a true record.

In 1991, an Italian expedition led by Oreste Forno traced a partially new route on the North Face. The itinerary passed along the Great Couloir, to the left of the 1984 Australian route, and directly tackled the rocky drop which bars the gully at 8,400 meters (passages of V degree, the only stretch secured with fixed ropes). Without the help of the Sherpas, without oxygen

and with three high altitude camps, at respectively 6,100, 6,195 and 7,600 meters, Battistino Bonali and the Czech Leopold Sulovsky reached the summit in the early afternoon of 17th May. A few days before, during another attempt, after two bivouacs at 8,000 and 8,350 meters, Fausto De Stefani had had a cerebral edema. With the help of his rope companion Giuliano De Marchi, and then with the aid of the whole expedition, De Stefani had however gained the foot of the mountain. In that same period, the success of the first Sherpa expedition was also recorded, directed by Lopsang and Tenzing Tashi along the South Col route.

122 bottom  August 31, 1986: photographed by Erhard Loretan, the Swiss climber Jean Troillet has just reached the summit of Everest together with his companion. The two climbers completed a very rapid ascent of the Japanese 1980 route on the North Face.
Photo: Archive
Jean Troillet

122-123  The immense and apparently impregnable North Face of Everest has over the years been scaled by various routes, some of them very direct.
Photo by Colin Monteath/ Hedgehog House

123 bottom  August 1986: the Swiss climber Erhard Loretan is about to abandon the summit. With a series of long slides; he reached the base of the North Face together with Jean Troillet in less than 5 hours.
Photo by Jean Troillet

124-125 The American climber Edward Webster climbing at the head of a rope party along an extremely steep wall of ice barring the route on the East Wall of Everest, one of the most impressive and difficult on the immense Himalayan mountain.

124 top Spring 1988: the Canadian Paul Teare tackling a section of vertical ice on a new, difficult route on the East Face of Everest, to the right of the spur scaled in 1983. None of the expedition's climbers used breathing gear.

*125 left* The British climber Robert Anderson, photographed by Stephen Venables, scaling a difficult pitch on the East Face of Everest. Venables reached the summit alone on the 12th of May. His slower-climbing companions surrendered near the South Summit.

*125 top right* Paul Teare crossing a large crevasse on the Kangshung side. The very difficult new route opened by the Anderson expedition emerged near Everest's South Col at around 8,000 meters.

*125 bottom right* The East Face of Everest: Paul Teare and Robert Anderson attempting to reach the South Col above Camp II. In the distance, at the bottom of the photo, can be seen the Kangshung Glacier. Photos by Stephen Venables/Agence Freestyle

126-127 Summer 1988, the "Esprit d'équipe" expedition: following an initial attempt that was foiled by the snow conditions, on the 13th of September the "Esprit d'équipe" group set out again along the Hornbein Couloir. However, the upper section of the gully was disappointing as the snow would not "hold."

*126 bottom left*
*If climbed in its entirety the Hornbein Couloir, named after the American climber who with a companion scaled the upper section in 1963, represents a route of rare beauty.*

*126 bottom right*
*A climber from a group led by Benoît Chamoux climbing in the Northern Cwm at the foot of the great North Face of Everest.*

*127 top A rope party ascending the steep slopes giving access to the Hornbein Couloir on the North Face. This climb was soon to be halted by bad weather.*

*127 bottom At an altitude of 8,500 meters on the slopes of the Hornbein Couloir, the Czechoslovakian climber Joska Rakoncaj begins to feel the fatigue caused by climbing too quickly.*

Photos by
Pascal Tournaire

*128 top left  A rope party climbing towards the North Col. The route indicated by the British pioneers of the 1920s is as valid today as ever, especially with the vast increase in the number of expeditions on the Tibetan side of the mountain.*
Photo by René Robert/ Agence Freestyle

*128 bottom left  A camp on the North Col, said the prewar Everest climbers, is like a bridge between two different worlds. Beyond the Chang-La saddle, in fact, opens the universe of ultra-high altitudes.*
Photo by René Robert/ Agence Freestyle

*128 right  The slopes overlooking the North Col are furrowed by the tracks of climbers and porters. However, high altitude winds or a day of sun are all it takes to eliminate all trace of their passing.*
Photo by Jean Michel Asselin/Agence Freestyle

*128-129 The great Everest pyramid and its two faces: on the left, the great North Face; in the center, the West Ridge; on the right the Southwest Face; below the West Shoulder.*
Photo by Jean Michel Asselin/Vertical

*129 bottom At 8,200 meters, the North Ridge of Everest appears to be suspended in the rarefied high altitude atmosphere, above a world of snow, rock and ice.*
Photo by Jean Michel Asselin/Vertical

*130-131 The shadow of the night seems to be struggling with the sun on the peaks of Everest, Lhotse and Nuptse. This is a memorable image, especially for those fortunate enough to observe it at first hand.*
Photo by Jean Michel Asselin/Vertical

131 top *The rays of the evening sun illuminate the Nepalese side of the great Everest pyramid and the clouds contribute to the magical, surreal atmosphere of the moment.* Photo by René Robert/ Agence Freestyle

131 bottom *A truly poetic image: the setting sun caresses Everest's North Col, emphasizing the elegant lines of the ridge.* Photo by René Robert/ Agence Freestyle

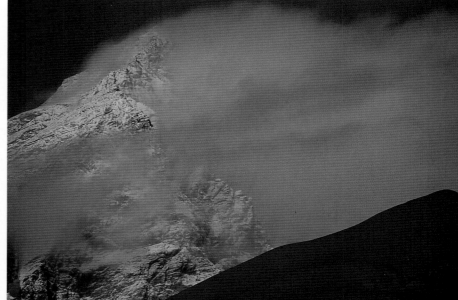

*132 During the 1990s the classic Everest routes have seen a remarkable increase in the number of expeditions. In the spring of 1993 no less than 40 climbers set foot on the world's highest peak in a single day.*

*133 top right The enormous crevasses and seracs of the Khumbu Ice Fall represent a veritable bastion defending Everest from excessive numbers of climbers.*

*133 center left Far from the base camp, the North Face of Everest still retains its wild spirit. The great wall continues to be a symbol for young climbers throughout the world.*

*133 center right Following the heavy monsoon snowfalls, at the end of the summer Everest has a new and even more impressive and majestic face that revives memories of the turn of the century pioneers.*

*133 bottom The summit crest of Everest, scaled for the first time by Hillary and Tenzing in May of 1953, should continue to be a place of dreams, a kind of interface between the real and the imaginary.*

Photos by
Pascal Tournaire

*134 top  The line of the ridges that converge on the North Col, set off by the unusual contrast of light and shadow, is incredibly beautiful at certain times of the day.*

*134 center  The snow, the freezing nights and above all the wind, continuously modify the form of the ridge that rises from Chang-La towards the northeast peak of Everest.*

*134 bottom  When visibility is good you can gaze from the North Col of Everest out towards Pumori, the beautiful peak rising in the west.*

*135  The photographer's eye has captured an image that truly does justice to the Everest myth. Here the lens of the camera points towards the slopes descending from the North Ridge above the North Col.*

Photos by Pat Morrow

*136 top  In 1991 an Italian expedition led by Oreste Forno opened a partially new route along the Great Couloir, to the left of the Australian route of 1984. In the photo Fausto De Stefani, a Himalayan climber of international renown with a large number of significant climbs to his name, climbs rapidly towards Camp IV.*

*136 bottom  Leopold Sulovsky played a significant part in the Italian expedition, devoting himself to the success of the venture.*

*136-137  Battistino Bonali climbing towards Camp II. Without making use of oxygen, early in the afternoon of the 17th of May he reached the summit of Everest together with Leopold Sulovsky.*

*137 bottom left The Czech Leopold Sulovsky, photographed whilst climbing towards Camp III.*

*137 bottom right The climber Fausto De Stefani is seen arriving at the tents of Camp III. Shortly afterwards, following two bivouacs at 8,000 and 8,350 meters he was struck by cerebral edema, fortunately without serious consequences.*

*137 top right  Battistino Bonali on the summit of Everest; alongside him is an oxygen bottle abandoned a few days earlier by a group of Sherpas who had climbed from Nepalese side.*

Photos by Oreste Forno

*138-139 A number of climbers ascending the slopes of the North Col in the spring of 1994. In the pre-monsoon season of that year innumerable expeditions ventured onto the slopes of Everest, some of them organized on a commercial basis.*

*138 bottom left Mountaineer Chantal Mauduit ascending a steep snow-covered slope during an attempt to open a new independent route on the Tibetan side of Everest.*

*138 bottom right 1994: The French climber Chantal Mauduit attempting a new route from the North Col, an increasingly difficult enterprise considering the number of routes already traced on the north side of Everest.*

In the last few years, climbing activity on Everest has become frenzied on both sides. Ascents have multiplied (by the end of 1996 there had been more than 800), as have attempts, and also the number of fatal accidents.

These years have also seen the appearance of the first commercial expeditions which, for a fee, accompany groups of customers to the summit. This is a phenomenon which, given its disastrous consequences, has led to much controversy.

Amidst the chaos of the various ascents, we may mention the first winter ascent of the Southwest Face in December 1993 by a Japanese expedition which in only three weeks succeeded in achieving the route. And also the official measuring of the summit by the "EV-K²-CNR" expedition in the autumn of 1992, which calculated 8,846.10 meters (8,848 on the snow

mantle). And lastly the partial descent on skis by Hans Kammerlander, on 24th May 1996, along the main line of the Northeast Ridge (obviously under it) and of the North Col. Before putting on his skis, the South Tyrolean mountaineer covered the traditional route on the Tibetan side in just 17 hours from the advance base camp at 6,500 meters.

It is however quite impossible to list all the more recent expeditions, often mere repetitions of the normal routes. An account of all the ascents and the dozens of attempts ending in failure would mean writing another book with many chapters all alike, a sort of long register of names, dates and summary technical details, which would risk further depreciating a story that is still full of fantasy and creativity. In any case, the events of the last few years must constitute a subject for serious reflection for all

# *THE CHAOS OF THE LAST SEASONS*

*139 top right  Everest rises majestically with its myriad secrets and continual challenges.*

*139 bottom  The climbers from the French expedition of 1994 emerge from their tents ready for another demanding day on the slopes of the Himalayan giant.*

Photos by René Robert/ Agence Freestyle

concerned. The heedless race to the summit by climbers without real experience, the fall in ethical values, the exasperating individualism and lack of solidarity are completely stifling the genuine spirit of Himalayan mountaineering. It is hard to hypothesize short-term improvements. But it is clear that things cannot go on like this. One solution might be to establish strict rules. But we do not have to be clairvoyants to see that rules and regulations cannot live alongside the spirit of mountaineering, especially in the high altitude world. It would be far preferable to promote self-regulation by the mountaineering community and to establish a new philosophy that is able to question not only the motives and behavior of climbers, but also the theoretic core of mountaineering itself. The penalty of failing to do this will be the death of a wonderful dream.

*140 top  The evening sun gilds the vast North Face of Everest, obscured below only by the shadow of nearby Changtse.*
Photo by Jean Michel Asselin/Vertical

*140 bottom  The spectacle of the setting sun sinking beneath the sea of clouds is one of the rarest and most beautiful to be seen from the summit of Everest.*
Photo by Pascal Tournaire

*141  From the top of the South Summit of Everest, the glacial basin of the Western Cwm appears to be at the bottom of a great abyss.*
Photo by Pascal Tournaire

*142-143  The sun rays illuminate the massive slopes of the Himalayan peaks that surround Everest, clearly visible in the background.*
Photo by Jean Michel Asselin/Vertical

*144 A Nepalese Sherpa,*
*engaged by the Canadian*
*expedition led by William*
*March, climbing towards*
*the summit of Everest*
*along the classic South*
*Col Route.*
Photo by Pat Morrow